Praying With Jesus

PAUL YONGGI CHO

Creation  **House**
Strang Communications Company
Altamonte Springs, FL 32714

Creation House
Strang Communications Company
190 N. Westmonte Drive
Altamonte Springs, FL 32714
(305) 869-5005

Unless otherwise noted, all Scripture quotations are from the
King James Version of the Bible.

First printing, January 1988
Second printing, March 1988

Contents

Foreword

What should we pray for and how?" The disciples of Jesus asked this question. But people who want to live by faith or who face desperate problems still ask it.

In answer to the question, Jesus gave us the perfect example in the Lord's prayer, found in Matthew 6:9-13. This prayer, which shows God's divine love, is not only an example for our prayer, but it is also the prayer we should pray for God to accomplish. Even if we simply memorize and quote the words by rote, this short prayer is full of powerful grace. If we go one step further and understand the meaning of each phrase, our prayer becomes bolder, our faith becomes stronger. We receive answers to our prayer and enjoy a deeper fellowship with God.

I trust that this small book which I present will be a helpful guide to all readers who desire to know how to pray as Jesus did:

Our Father which art in heaven, Hallowed be thy name. Thy kingdom come. Thy will be done in earth, as it is in heaven. Give us this day our daily bread. And forgive us our debts, as we forgive our debtors. And lead us not into temptation, but deliver us from evil. For thine is the kingdom, and the power, and the glory, for ever.
Amen.

1

Our Father Which Art in Heaven

What is prayer? In short, it is a dialogue with God in which our attitudes and thoughts are grafted into God's thoughts. If we are to pray effectively, we must condition our thoughts to divine thoughts, and our attitudes must be right in relation to God's. Whether or not our right thoughts are actually verbalized, they are a savory offering pleasing to God. But how can we judge whether or not our thoughts are right in God's eyes? Our standard of measure is the Word of God.

In the Bible, God wrote down His thoughts. When we read the Scriptures with open hearts, making our thoughts fit the Word and putting our hope in Him, God will answer our prayer according to what His good will desires.

Jesus gave the Lord's prayer as the most significant summation of the Word.

The prayer Jesus taught us is the right thinking we must implant in our hearts: God becomes our Father; His kingdom comes upon our hearts, into our lives and into this world; God fills all our daily needs; He keeps us from evil and does not lead us into temptation; He forgives our sins and delivers us from evil.

Jesus prayed what has become known as "the Lord's Prayer" in response to His disciples' request for a lesson in prayer, and the points Jesus covered are significant as a model for our own thoughts in relation to God.

At the very beginning of the prayer Jesus taught, He clearly laid the groundwork for the proper attitude we should have toward God: "Our Father which art in heaven." He is One to whom we can confide the earnest desire of our hearts through our right thoughts. Only He can hear our prayer and answer it. God is waiting for us to have the same thoughts as His. Let's look at what the Word says about our Father in heaven.

Our Father

While I was conducting a crusade in the United States, I received a letter from a divorcee who cited the difficulties of raising her children without a father. As I read the letter I was reminded of how important a father's role is to his children.

When Jesus taught, He referred to God as "Father." In the Sermon on the Mount alone Jesus called God "Father" seventeen times. Why do you think Jesus commanded us to call God "Father"?

How Has God Become Our Father?
In the beginning God made Adam and Eve His children.

God made them according to His own image and breathed breath—or the Spirit—into them. Because of their divine image and spirit, Adam and Eve's thoughts and character were just like those of God. As a father knew what was in the mind of his son and the son knew what was in the mind of his father, so God knew what was in the mind of Adam and Eve; Adam and Eve knew what was in the mind of God.

Referring to His sons and daughters, God said, "Every one that is called by my name...I have created him for my glory" (Is. 43:7). When children behave well, parents receive honor. But when children behave shamefully, parents receive dishonor. God wanted Adam and Eve— whom He made according to His own image and likeness and into whom He breathed His Spirit—to give Him glory and honor forever.

But Adam and Eve refused to remain the children of God; they volunteered to become the children of Satan. When they broke the commandment of God, a curse was immediately pronounced, and their spirits died. In Ezekiel 18:4 God said, "Behold, all souls are mine; as the soul of the father, so also the soul of the son is mine: the soul that sinneth, it shall die."

Adam and Eve, whose spirits had died because of sin, could no longer enjoy dialogue with God; nor could they please Him, nor could they glorify Him. The divine image was no more found in fallen humanity.

But God did not give up because He is love (1 John 4:8). (It takes more than one person to make love work. Love is possible only when there is one who is loved by another. The Father is the One who loves; Jesus is the One who is loved; and the Holy Spirit is the One who conveys love. So God makes the complete Trinity in love.) And He always wants to give His overflowing love to as many children as possible.

9

Jesus expressed this when He said, "O Jerusalem, Jerusalem, thou that killest the prophets, and stonest them which are sent unto thee, how often would I have gathered thy children together, even as a hen gathered her chickens under her wings, and you would not!" (Matt. 23:37).

Such divine love caused God to clothe Adam and Eve with the skins of an animal which He had killed. The shedding of this blood foreshadowed God's willingness to forgive and cover the sins and trespasses of mankind by making God the holy Son die on the cursed tree, the cross. Throughout the 4,000 years of the Old Testament, God promised and confirmed again and again that He would send Christ.

Since the fall of Adam no human being could appear before the righteous God. Any righteous act has failed to free mankind of sin. Because of the earnest love of God to make us again His children and become our Father, God sent His Son to this world that He might die as the eternal Lamb of atonement.

Since mankind's spirit was dead because of the fall, humanity was merely good-for-nothing dust. But Jesus voluntarily died to fulfill the divine love and to impart the foreordained grace of God. What was the divine will Jesus accomplished as He died, declaring His last word, "It is finished" (John 19:30)? Jesus Himself answers the question: "And this is the will of him that sent me, that everyone which seeth the Son, and believeth on him, may have everlasting life: and I will raise him up at the last day" (John 6:40).

What then is everlasting life? It is eternal life which God gives. It was the life Adam and Eve received from God before their fall into sin. The night before His trial and death, Jesus said, "And this is life eternal, that they might know thee the only true God, and Jesus Christ, whom thou hast sent" (John 17:3).

When we believe in Jesus as Messiah or our Savior, we have everlasting life. When we have everlasting life— namely the life of God through rebirth of water and of the Spirit—we get to know God. Our spirit is quickened. When we receive everlasting life, we receive the Spirit of adoption, whereby we call God, "Abba, Father" (Rom. 8:15). At such a moment, "the Spirit itself beareth witness with our spirit, that we are the children of God" (Rom. 8:16), for God "hath sealed us, and given the earnest of the Spirit in our hearts" (2 Cor. 1:22).

With great eloquence the apostle Paul wrote about the will of God to make us His children: "Blessed be the God and Father of our Lord Jesus Christ, who hath blessed us with all spiritual blessings in heavenly places in Christ...Having predestined us unto the adoption of children by Jesus Christ to himself, according to the good pleasure of his will, to the praise of the glory of his grace, wherein he hath made us accepted in the beloved" (Eph. 1:3,5,6).

By faith in Jesus through which our spirit is quickened, we become the children of God. When we eat the torn flesh of Jesus and drink the blood Jesus shed for us, we have eternal life with us (John 5:54). Jesus has become our righteousness and everyone who relies on Him can boldly stand before Him (Heb. 10:19). Because of His love, God made us His children and paid the price for it.

God, who has opened the way for us to become His children, wants everyone to have eternal life and become His children. It is not we, but God who has redeemed us from our sin. God has fulfilled all the conditions necessary for us to have everlasting life and to become the children of God.

All we have to do is to believe unconditionally, to confess with our mouths that Jesus is the Son of God and that our sins are forgiven by His crucifixion. Jesus said that "whosoever believeth in him should not perish, but have everlasting life" (John 3:16). He also said, "As many as received him to them gave he power to become the sons of God, even to them that believe on his name: which were born, not of blood, nor of the will of the flesh, nor of the will of man, but of God" (John 1:12,13). It was the good pleasure of God to make believers His children in this way (Eph. 1:5).

God had a great plan to make us His children. By sending His only begotten Son, Jesus, to this world and making Him die, God has prepared the way so we can call God "Father." He also gave us the boldness to call Him "Father" by sending us the Spirit of adoption.

Thus we have become the children of God a second time. The first time we became His children by creation and the second time we were bought with the price of blood. God's purpose in creation and in redemption was the same: He wants us to praise the grace He has shown us. As long as we praise the grace of God and give Him glory, there is nothing that can sever us from the love of Christ. As Jesus said, "And I give unto them eternal life; and they shall never perish, neither shall any man pluck them out of my hand. My Father, which gave them me, is greater than all; and no man is able to pluck them out of my Father's hand" (John 10:28,29).

Our relationship to God as His children by virtue of the blood of Jesus is a spiritual blood tie. There is no one who can sever that tie—neither in this world nor in the world to come.

Approaching Our Father

Jesus said that we should call God, "our Father." The proper thoughts we should have when we call God "our Father" are as follows:

12

As we center our thoughts on God our Father we must always keep in mind the precious blood of Jesus. The fact that we are saved does not mean that we are able to stand before God without the merit of the precious blood. The song with which we shall praise God forever concerns the power of the blood. The futuristic vision that the apostle John saw on the Island of Patmos included the redeemed saints in heaven praising Jesus the Lamb: "Thou art worthy to take the book, and to open the seals thereof: for thou wast slain, and hast redeemed us to God by the blood out of every kindred, and tongue, and people, and nation; and hast made us unto our God kings and priests: and we shall reign on the earth" (Rev. 5:9,10).

In that same vision John saw the great multitude of saints, saved by the preaching of the 144,000 Israelites, standing before the throne and the Lamb and crying out, "Salvation to our God which sitteth upon the throne, and unto the Lamb" (Rev. 7:10).

Because we will eternally sing of the blood of Jesus to commemorate our salvation, when we pray, "Our Father which art in heaven," we must remember that God is the Father of Jesus at the same time He is our Father. When Jesus first showed His resurrected body to Mary Magdalene after He had fulfilled the will of God to make us His children by dying on the cross, He said, "Go to my brethren, and say unto them, I ascend unto my Father, and your Father; and to my God, and your God" (John 20:17). Without hesitation, Jesus called His disciples brothers. His Father became the Father of the disciples; His God became the God of the disciples.

We had not been able to call God our Father until Jesus gave us the privilege. When we call God "our Father" we must also remember that He is the Father of all believers who are united by the presence of Jesus Christ

13

in their hearts. Everyone who worships God, praises God, believes in Jesus as Savior and recognizes and welcomes the Holy Spirit as the Comforter is a brother or sister in God. We are the building materials of the spiritual temple in which God dwells. Jesus said, "Where two or three are gathered together in my name, there am I in the midst of them" (Matt. 18:20).

God dwells within us through the Holy Spirit making us His temple (1 Cor. 3:16). In his letter to the Ephesians, Paul said, "In whom [Christ] all the building fitly framed together groweth unto an holy temple in the Lord: in whom ye also are builded together for an habitation of God through the spirit" (Eph. 2:21, 22). Our brothers and sisters in the Lord should be united to build the house of God upon the foundation of the life, death and resurrection of Christ, keeping it clean so the Spirit of God may dwell therein.

When we call God "our Father," we should also think of our unbelieving neighbors who have not come to the Lord. They need to hear our witness of the Father's love. It is the will of God that all who hear the gospel should believe it. And all who believe it shall have everlasting life. God puts no other conditions or restrictions on our salvation.

God clearly says, "And the Spirit and the bride say, Come. And let him that heareth say, Come. And let him that is athirst come. And whosoever will, let him take the water of life freely" (Rev. 22:17).

Before He ascended into heaven, Jesus said to His disciples, "But ye shall receive power, after that the Holy Ghost is come upon you: and ye shall be witnesses unto me both in Jerusalem, and in all Judea, and in Samaria, and unto the uttermost part of the earth" (Acts 1:8). God wants all people to become His children and He gives the power for us to share the good news.

Which Art in Heaven

As we speak to God our Father, we should have right thoughts about where He is. We should remove the notion that He is in a vaguely defined, far-off place and replace that thought with a specific picture of where He dwells—in terms of both space and time. In Isaiah 43:10 God says that He wants us to know Him in minute detail, so let's consider what we know about His dwelling and being.

Where Is God?

Since the fall of Adam and Eve no one has been able to know God by himself. Because of sin, the way to know God was severed. Unless God manifests Himself today, no one can know Him.

Nearly three decades ago when I first read the Bible after I had opened my heart to the gospel, I was greatly moved by the ministry and love of Jesus. Yet a question bothered me. As I saw it, the miracles of Jesus happened 2,000 years ago in the land of Judea. They had nothing to do with me—living now and in the Far East. The Bible I was reading seemed no more than a book of historical events. What connection did I have with a book written 2,000 years ago for the Jews?

Question after question arose and confused me, yet I kept reading to find an answer that could lead me out of my doubt. I even had imaginary talks with the great figures who had seen God. Maybe that would give me more insight, I reasoned.

I first sought Adam, the progenitor of the human race. "Father Adam," I asked, "where did you meet God?"

Adam answered, "You can meet Him in the Garden of Eden. I always had a talk with Him there in the cool of the evening."

15

"But aren't you banished from that place? And isn't it true that no one can have access to it?" When I asked this, Adam just stood silently and bowed his head. Unable to find a satisfactory answer, I went to Abraham, the father of believers. "Abraham, since you always walked with God, can you tell me where God is?"

"Whenever I wanted to meet God," he answered, "I built up an altar, offered an animal sacrifice and waited. Sometimes He showed Himself quickly but other times not so quickly. Only at the altar did I meet Him. I don't know where He is now."

Then I went to Moses, the great servant of the Lord who obeyed God and delivered the Israelites from Egypt. "Moses," I asked, "didn't you meet God in a flame of fire burning in a bush on Mount Horeb? And didn't you also meet Him at the top of Mount Sinai? Surely you can tell me where God is."

"God dwelt in the tabernacle we had built. I always met Him before the mercy seat in the tabernacle, but I don't know where He is now."

Still dissatisfied, I went to King Solomon. "King Solomon, you are the one who built the temple where God could dwell. So can you tell me where He is now?"

"Of course God dwelt in the temple I built. People always came there to pray and they received answers. Even when they were in a strange country, they received answers if they prayed turning their faces toward the temple."

"O King, but didn't the temple fall 2,600 years ago at the invasion of Assyria and Babylon?"

Unable to find a definite answer from King Solomon either, I went to John the Baptist. "John, where is the God you met?" I asked.

"Behold, the Lamb of God, which takes away the sin of the world," he answered. "God is in Jesus."

Feeling my heart excited, I started reading the Gospels—from Matthew through Mark and Luke to John. Then I knelt down humbly before Jesus and asked, "Jesus, let me know where God is now."

With the help of the Holy Spirit I read the scriptures that were written as an answer to that question:

> Jesus said unto him, I am the way, the truth, and the life: no man cometh unto the Father, but by me. If ye had known me, ye should have known my Father also: and from henceforth ye know him, and have seen him. Philip saith unto him, Lord, shew us the Father...Jesus saith unto him, Have I been so long time with you, and yet hast thou not known me, Philip? he that hath seen me hath seen the Father; and how sayest thou then, Shew us the Father? Believest thou not that I am in the Father, and the Father in me? The words that I speak unto you I speak not of myself: but the Father that dwelleth in me, he doeth the works. Believe me that I am in the Father, and the Father in me: or else believe me for the very works' sake (John 14:6-11).

When I heard the voice of Jesus through this scripture, the light of truth began to shine in my heart; the clouds of doubt began to disappear. But I wasn't completely free of the doubt. I asked again, "Lord Jesus, when You were in this world, people met God the Father and saw His works through You. But since You were crucified, died, rose again and ascended into heaven we can't meet God. Where is God at this hour—now?"

Jesus answered me by bringing another scripture to my mind and heart:

> And I will pray the Father, and he shall give you

17

another Comforter, that he may abide with you for ever; even the Spirit of truth; whom the world cannot receive, because it seeth him not, neither knoweth him: but ye know him; for he dwelleth with you, and shall be in you. I will not leave you comfortless: I will come to you. Yet a little while, and the world seeth me no more; but ye see me: because I live, ye shall live also. At that day ye shall know that I am in my Father, and ye in me, and I in you (John 14:16-20).

This word of Jesus instantly led me into the light, for through this scripture I learned that when I had received Jesus in my heart as Savior—accepting salvation by washing of the precious blood of Jesus—God the Father and His Son had both come in me through the Holy Spirit. From that moment on I resolutely resisted the temptations of the devil. God in my heart dispersed the clouds of doubt. As Jesus said, "If a man love me, he will keep my words: and my Father will love him, and we will come unto him, and make our abode with him" (John 14:23).

The apostles emphasized again and again that God is with us. If we asked the apostle Paul where God is, he would probably say, "Know ye not that ye are the temple of God, and that the Spirit of God dwelleth in you?" (1 Cor. 3:16). And John would probably answer, "Ye are of God, little children, and have overcome them: because greater is he that is in you, than he that is in the world" (1 John 4:4).

Then where is God within us? The Bible reads, "Who hath also sealed us, and given the earnest of the Spirit in our hearts" (2 Cor. 1:22). God is in the midst of our hearts through the Holy Spirit. And since He is in the midst of our hearts, our hearts become the kingdom of

18

heaven. As Jesus said, "The kingdom of God is within you" (Luke 17:21). The name Immanuel actually means "God with us."

Is our heart then the only dwelling place of God? No. If it were, the biblical promise concerning the heavenly home we will some day enter would be void. Jesus certainly said, "I go to prepare a place for you. And if I go and prepare a place for you, I will come again, and receive you unto myself; that where I am, there ye may be also" (John 14:2,3). Mark recorded, "So then after the Lord [Jesus] had spoken unto them, he was received up into heaven, and sat on the right hand of God" (Acts 7:56). The writer of Hebrews also witnessed Jesus who was "set down at the right hand of the throne of God" (Heb. 12:2). In addition, the apostle John described heaven, where God was, in great detail as he wrote down his vision. All this goes to show that God will eventually unfold His eternal kingdom in a place called heaven that is hidden to us; He will bring us there to live with Him forever. Why then has God come to this earth and why is He dwelling in our hearts?

Since God is righteous and holy, no unrighteous member of the fallen human race could stand before Him. Nobody could know about God, since mankind's spirit died when Adam fell. Even the greatest scholar today is like a blind man when it comes to the knowledge of God. Unless God allows us to know Him, eye cannot see, nor can ear hear, neither will it enter into the heart of man, the things which God has prepared for them that love him (1 Cor. 2:9).

Jesus has come to earth in the form of human flesh to reveal God to us and to accomplish God's will—to deliver us from sin and make us His children. If we are forgiven of our sins, born again by the power of the blood of Jesus, He enters our hearts and dwells therein through the Holy

Spirit. From this moment on we become the children of God and the citizens of heaven. If we are citizens of heaven, we also receive and enjoy the blessings God has prepared for us.

Our God keeps and raises the children whom He has bought with the price of the blood of His only begotten Son. He gives increase to them and makes them bear fruit. When we pray to "Our Father which art in heaven," we must think of Him as the God who rules from His throne in heaven, who sealed with the Holy Spirit those who believe in His Son, making them His children, and who dwells in our hearts and will lead us into heaven to glorify us. Such a God is our Father!

God in Relation to the Present, Past and Future

To which time period does God belong? Some people contend that God worked in the past but doesn't do anything now. Voltaire, the French philosopher, maintained that God created this world as a clockmaker would make a perfect clock; however, He no longer does anything to the world because everything works well according to the laws He set in motion.

Some theologians have maintained that this God, who gave revelation, performed miracles and worked among us at one time, is dead. They assert that this world would become a better place to live in by only human wisdom and the social system that man invented.

In the light of the Word of God, let's examine how their assertion is false and evil. "And God said moreover unto Moses, Thus shalt thou say unto the children of Israel, The Lord God of your fathers, the God of Abraham, the God of Isaac, and the God of Jacob, hath sent me unto you: this is my name for ever, and this is my memorial unto all generations" (Ex. 3:15).

This passage shows that the God of Abraham was the

God of Isaac, Abraham's son, and the God of Jacob, Abraham's grandson. He also became the God of Moses and of the people of Israel in the time of Moses. God said, "For I am the Lord, I change not; therefore ye sons of Jacob are not consumed" (Mal. 3:6). To His faithful in the Old Testament God was always the God of the present. The God of Abraham was the God of Samuel; the God of Samuel was the God of Solomon and the God of Daniel.

Is God then only the God of the Old Testament but not God of the New Testament? On the fourth day after Lazarus, the brother of Martha, died, Jesus came to Bethany where they lived. Martha fell upon her face before Jesus and complained, weeping, "Lord, if thou hadst been here, my brother had not died."

Martha trusted the power of Jesus—in the past tense—but Jesus said, "Thy brother shall rise again."

"I know that he shall rise again in the resurrection at the last day." Martha recognized Jesus of the past and Jesus of the future, but she couldn't recognize the Jesus of the present who was going to perform a miracle before her eyes. Jesus said with a sigh, "I am the resurrection, and the life: he that believeth in me, though he were dead, yet shall he live: and whosoever liveth and believeth in me shall never die. Believest thou this?" (John 11:21-26).

God, whom we call "our Father," is of the past; He created this world. At the same time He is God of the present; He holds everything in His power, daily operating it according to His will. And He is also the God of the future. He is our everlasting God. Just before Jesus ascended into heaven to the right hand of God the Father, He said, "Lo, I am with you alway, even unto the end of the world" (Matt. 28:20). As everything Jesus promised to us comes to pass daily in our lives, we realize that this saying of our Lord is an unfailing truth.

Even after Jesus ascended, the apostles always wrote about the God of the present: "Now unto him that is able to do exceeding abundantly above all that we ask or think, according to the power that worketh in us" (Eph. 3:20). "For it is God which worketh in you both to will and to do of his good pleasure" (Phil. 2:13). "Jesus Christ the same yesterday, and today, and for ever" (Heb. 13:8).

In addition, from the apostolic age to the present, millions of forefathers in the faith have walked with the God of the present until they have been called to heaven. Our Father *is* the living God who is the same yesterday and today and forever.

When God Becomes Our Father

Have you ever thought of the charge that comes and the blessing we receive when we, who were dead in spirit, are quickened through our faith in the power of the blood of Christ? Have you ever tasted of infinite joy and eternal hope? Have you ever experienced boldness as firm as a rock?

God, our good Father, is far better than any earthly father no matter how fine and beautiful his qualities.

When we center our thoughts upon God the Father, we sense His love and fathering abilities. A father admonishes us with love. He encourages us and has expectations of us. He forgives us and comforts us when we are in trouble. God becomes such a father to us—and more: He is the Father of righteousness and the Father of love; He is also the Father of power and providence. When Jesus introduced to us God the Father, He used a dramatic example:

What man is there of you, whom if his son ask bread,

22

will he give him a stone? Or if he ask a fish, will he give him a serpent? If ye then, being evil, know how to give good gifts unto your children, how much more shall your Father which is in heaven give good things to them that ask him? (Matt. 7:9-11).

Close your eyes for a moment and think about the parable of the prodigal son. Imagine the scene of the son heading toward his childhood home. As you remember, he had been an undutiful son, a selfish brother. Because he had wasted all his inheritance, he endured a miserable life and the scorn and contempt of villagers he passed by. Several times a day he suppressed the urge to turn around and go back or just give up, but he kept walking, nearer and nearer to his father's house. Finally he got to the edge of his hometown. He felt as if he heard the whispers of the villagers—mocking him like the sound of rushing water; he felt as if he were seeing their scornful looks—like the scorching sunlight.

But when he actually reached the entrance of the village, he was greeted by his father, standing there with open arms. The first person the prodigal son met was not a talkative woman of the village, nor was it his legalistic elder brother. It was none other than his loving, merciful father who was driven by the affection of a father for his son. Seeing the pathetic appearance of his son, the father ran to him, fell on his neck and kissed him. The son, pricked by a guilty conscience, was humbled; he begged his father to hire him as one of the servants. Yet to the boy's surprise, the father ordered the servants to clothe him in the best robe, put a ring on his finger and shoes on his swollen feet. He had a calf killed and called for a feast.

In a loud voice the father announced to the villagers, "Let us eat, and be merry: for this my son was dead, and is alive again; he was lost, and he is found" (Luke 15:23,24). Then they heartily celebrated the restoration of father and son. The renewed relationship between them was started by the father who had called him "my son."

A similar dramatic encounter takes place between God and us. We do not first call God "Father"; God first calls us "children." This is the grace of God who gives to us freely—not expecting anything in return. What does God, our Father, give to His children?

God Sets Us Free

If we, through the Holy Spirit, call God "Father" and go to His bosom as the prodigal son went to the bosom of his father, we are set free from uneasiness and fear— the enemies that can paralyze a person and destroy human life. The devil walks about like a roaring lion to put uneasiness and fear in the human heart.

One kind of modern warfare is psychological. Its tactic is to plant uneasiness in the mind of the enemy so they will surrender even before the physical combat begins. Our enemy, the devil, also stages psychological warfare against us.

In the first stage, one's peace of mind is broken. One thinks vaguely about negative things. After a while, one imagines the negative more clearly. Uneasiness turns to fear. If one stays fearful for a while, that person feels as if these things were really happening. This is the stage of terror—an emotion that arises when one can clearly identify the object of one's fear. These three stages may occur over a long period of time. But sometimes they happen almost simultaneously.

When we are thus terrified, we confess negative thoughts with our mouths. If we say, "I can't do it," or "I'm up a tree," or "It's impossible for me," we are

24

already finished in our hearts even though nothing has actually happened. If we have given in and accepted a negative result, it is only a matter of time before real failure takes over.

Uneasiness also takes away our happiness and health. Dr. Walter Clement Alberk, a specialist in gastroenteric disorders at Mayo Clinic in Minnesota, says that most diarrhea cases are caused by uneasiness. Proverbs 18:14 says, "The spirit of a man will sustain his infirmity; but a wounded spirit who can bear?" This means that when we keep our hearts in peace, when we have courage, the sickness of our bodies is quickly healed. Conversely, if our hearts become ill, there is no cure; as a consequence, we develop more serious problems.

Where then did such destructive emotions start? Uneasiness and fear were the emotions Adam and Eve felt when they sinned. Adam and Eve once maintained a close dialogue with God. But when they gave in to the temptation of Satan and ate the fruit of the tree of knowledge in violation of a divine command, fear surged into their hearts. They could not meet God as usual; among the trees of the garden they hid themselves from the presence of God. And when God called to Adam and said, "Where art thou?" he said, "I heard thy voice in the garden, and I was afraid, because I was naked; and I hid myself" (Gen. 3:9,10). Uneasiness and fear are not emotions God originally implanted in the human heart. They are the destructive emotions Satan brought into the world through sin.

Adam and Eve turned their backs against the Father in heaven. Consequently their offspring to this day have lived in the midst of uneasiness and fear. Until we call God "Father" we have a guilty conscience and misgivings of being condemned. Many try to rationalize and justify themselves by saying "I am clean" or "I am conscientious" because they are tormented by guilty consciences. In other words they struggle to release themselves from the apprehension of being condemned.

Those who turn their backs on God also tremble with fear which comes from an underlying sense of meaninglessness. People ask themselves, "Where did we come from?," "What are we living for?" or "Where will we go after death?" Some ask, "What good really is the better living, more time and more money? What does it mean?"

When I conduct crusades in countries that enjoy a high standard of living I often meet people who are in agony over such questions. Most of them are in their forties; they've achieved social status and a stable living. Unanimously, they ask, "Pastor Cho, I am tired of the daily routine at my workplace. I am disillusioned by my family life. I have lost my will to live. What shall I do now?" They writhe in the emptiness of their hearts because they have run with all their might for more than twenty years with a notion that they would be happy if they only got position, honor, power and wealth. But they find to their great frustration when they achieve those things that happiness is still far away. Meaninglessness has overtaken them like a tidal wave.

An apprehension about death also covers human beings. Every human being is born with the destiny to die. Standing at the door of death, anyone who is not prepared to face death cannot help but to quake in fear. No one knows the time of his death, but who over the age of forty hasn't thought about the possibility? When people attend funerals, they think that it might soon be themselves. Anxiety about death can be an undercurrent that flows through an unbeliever's thoughts.

People also feel uneasy about the future. What will happen to them? Will they be powerless in the face of some overwhelming problems?

During World War II, 300,000 young Americans were killed. But the number of U.S. citizens who died of a heart attack caused by anxiety, worry and apprehension because their sons and husbands were sent to the front is said to be more than one million. Apprehension and fear killed three times more people than the bullets!

The underlying cause of the Great Panic of the 1930s was uneasiness in the hearts of the American people. A rumor spread: "A great panic is coming. The bonds will become worthless paper. You can't draw your savings from the bank because it will cause a short in the reserves." People rushed to the banks and drew all their savings. When the banks closed down, firms had to shut down; millions of jobless people were driven out into the streets—as a result of apprehension.

How then can we be set free from such apprehension, fear and dread? When God becomes our Father, our apprehension leaves—like the mist that disappears with the morning sunlight. We become free from the chains of apprehension and we have peace and tranquility like the Sea of Galilee, the tempest of which was calmed.

We are set free from the apprehension of a guilty conscience and condemnation through the blood Jesus shed for us, redeeming our sins on the cross. Satan can no more have dominion over us, nor can he accuse us. Through our faith in and dependence on the blood of Jesus, God has become our Father and we are justified. In other words, we have acquired the righteous state and are not tainted with any sin.

How are we set free from the emptiness that comes when we feel as if life is meaningless? When God becomes our Father, the purpose of life becomes clear: We live to give glory to God.

God made us according to His will and predestined us to Himself according to the good pleasure of His will

(Eph. 1:5); He wants us to fulfill His will and eventually go to the home He has prepared for us. Jesus introduced God the Father as "Lord of heaven and earth" (Matt. 11:25). There is no reason why we who have such a God as our Father should feel as if life is meaningless.

When God becomes our Father, we are also set free from the fear of death. Though our bodies die, our spirits go to the kingdom of our heavenly Father. The death of the physical body is the beginning of the new life we have in the heavenly kingdom.

Jesus said, "In my Father's house are many mansions" (John 14:2), which God has prepared for His faithful. In the future, at His appointed time, God will raise His children from the dead that they may attend the marriage supper of the Lamb in heaven. Therefore we can cry boldly, "O death, where is thy sting? O grave, where is thy victory?" (1 Cor. 15:55).

Our Father also sets us free from the apprehension of the unknown future. God, whom we come to know through Jesus, is perfect, and He leads us into all truth through the Holy Spirit, our Comforter. Since we have become His children according to the good pleasure of His will, He makes everything work together for our benefit. In the Old Testament, God led Abraham into a world totally foreign to him. In the form of a pillar of fire and a pillar of cloud, He led the people of Israel to Canaan. Today, when we call God our Father and love Him, He still leads us with similar pillars—of peace and joy through the Holy Ghost.

As we face the problems that seem bigger than ourselves, we need only remember that God is the Father of hope and the Lord of power. When God, who made heaven and earth, becomes our Father, there is nothing we cannot do through our faith in Him.

Jesus made us to know our heavenly Father as an

always-working Father. Just as Jesus said, "My Father worketh hitherto, and I work," we too must work diligently for the glory of God with the power He gives to us.

The prophet Jeremiah was shut up in a deep pit in the courtyard of a prison. Maybe he deplored his inability to do something about his condition, but during this time the most powerful word of God came to him: "Thus saith the Lord the maker thereof, the Lord that formed it, to establish it; the Lord is his name; call unto me, and I will answer thee, and shew thee great and mighty things, which thou knowest not" (Jer. 33:2,3).

The Bible also reads, "For it is God which worketh in you both to will and to do of his good pleasure" (Phil. 2:13). Because of this promise, we can be confident in the face of any adversity.

Since we are born, not of blood nor of the will of the flesh nor of the will of man but of God, our Father is obliged to feed, clothe, bring up and educate us. When we sincerely cry to our Father, all the apprehension and fear Satan puts on us will disappear; in its place, peace and joy will overflow like a spring. The Bible clearly reads, "For as many as are led by the Spirit of God, they are the sons of God. For ye have not received the spirit of bondage again to fear; but ye have received the Spirit of adoption, whereby we cry, Abba, Father. The Spirit itself beareth witness with our spirit, that we are the children of God" (Rom. 8:14-16). "Let your conversation be without covetousness; and be content with such things as ye have: for he hath said, I will never leave thee, nor forsake thee. So that we may boldly say, The Lord is my helper, and I will not fear what man shall do unto me" (Heb. 13:5,6).

If God becomes our Father, we don't have to fear anything in this world. The first blessing Jesus lets us have when we pray, "Our Father which art in heaven," is this deliverance from apprehension.

God Makes Us Triumph

When we call God Father, we can be set free from any feeling of inferiority and frustration that is deeply rooted in our hearts; we can triumph in life.

Life itself is a struggle, from childhood through adulthood. And life is made more difficult when we compare ourselves with others. So often we are disappointed in ourselves and feel inferior to others who wear better clothes than ours, who live in better houses than ours, who have more ability than we have.

We know better than anyone else that most of our language, thought and behavior reflects our inferiority feelings. But the more we know, the more anguish and discord we suffer.

Persistent low self-esteem results in melancholia, which can cause one to abandon oneself to despair or resort to destructive behavior. Some people destroy themselves with drugs and alcohol, even to the ultimate extreme of suicide. For others, destructive behavior is seen in relationships: One woman who was a prisoner of an inferiority complex left her home, husband and children; another gave up her nursing baby.

Many criminals go on killing and hurting others because of their low self-esteem. Sometimes we plot against others and tear them into pieces—so we can hope to look better than they.

Where on earth does such destructive behavior come from? The fundamental cause of an inferiority complex is lack of love. The German philosopher Johann Fichte once said, "Love is the principal ingredient of man." Those who experience a lack of love as a child are prone to illness because of undernourishment in mind and body. And real happiness eludes them.

No amount of wealth, power and honor can fill our need for love. Most inmates in prisons are suffering a love deficiency. During their childhood they did not receive enough parental love. A person who hasn't felt real love is unable to love others, but more than that, that person can't love self either. And a person who cannot love self lacks confidence in everything. One or two mistakes, which ordinary people would take in stride, can disappoint an unloved person so that he thinks he is incompetent beyond remedy. I heard of a girl who burned herself to death after she had failed her college entrance examination three times. If she only could have held on to the love of God! Since Adam was driven out of the Garden of Eden, men and women have fallen away from the love of God, the ultimate source of love.

How can we be free from such feelings of inferiority and the disappointment that comes when we don't measure up? When God becomes our Father, miracles happen. When we recognize that the greatest One of this world really loved us, our inferiority complex and frustration disappear like fog.

The love between a man and a woman or the love between friends sometimes gives us encouragement and comfort. But such love is subject to change. From our parents we receive deeper and wider love. But these earthly loves fail us when a critical moment comes— when we are taken ill with a grave disease, when we face death, when we are physically separated from the source of love.

One day a young woman came to my office. She was a college graduate and attractive, but a chill shade hovered over her unsmiling face.

She shared her situation: "Pastor, I am an unhappy woman. When I attended college I was enticed by a

31

certain man's affectionate words. I surrendered my chastity to him, but he kept putting off our wedding day. Eventually I became suspicious and investigated his background. I unearthed the fact that he was a married man, even the father of a baby. I was living with him and continued my double life, as I had nowhere else to go, but my joy and smiles disappeared. I avoided the eyes of my parents, brothers and sisters. I avoided my classmates. He started coming home later and later at night, and finally he started staying away. Eventually I found out that in the meantime he had divorced his wife and married another woman. I felt destroyed, with neither the hope nor the energy to keep on living. My only concern was how I could end my feeble life—and his. These days I carry a dagger in my bosom. As soon as I find him I will stab his heart and then kill myself. I am that kind of a woman. I'm here because a friend strongly advised me to meet you. Pastor, is there any hope for someone like me?"

There was danger in her eyes. Anger and disappointment were mingled with confusion. What she said was true: It seemed as if destruction was the only thing left for her.

She had little faith in any male. "Being a man yourself," she said, "you'll probably side with him, won't you?"

I answered, "Sister, men and women are all the same before God. They are all strangers and pilgrims in this life. At the moment, I don't have the right words to give you full satisfaction and hope. But I can say one thing, and whether you accept this or not is your own choice: The God who created heaven and earth and you still loves you. And we who believe in Jesus love you, too.

"Now let me tell you one thing you can do. When you return home, before you go to bed, sit down before your dressing table. Look at yourself in the mirror and say to yourself, 'God still loves me!' When you get up in the morning, sit down in front of the dressing table again and cry, 'You stupid person. You wretched person! Nevertheless, God loves you.' If your tears run, never mind. Just let them flow. If your voice becomes loud, just keep on crying as loudly as you can. Close your eyes and imagine a picture of yourself being embraced by God in Jesus Christ. Imagine that Jesus is straightening out your sinful, unrighteous, ugly, deserted and crushed life, washing it out clean. See the picture of yourself, newly changed according to your drawing.''

Some time passed before the woman came to my office again. As soon as she sat down, she began to sob. She placed in front of me a dagger wrapped in a bandage, and she said, "I did what you told me. I figured it couldn't hurt—my life seemed so poor and miserable anyway. Every morning and evening I sat down at the dressing table. Through tears I said, 'God loves you anyway.' I pictured Jesus embracing me and smoothing my crumpled and ugly life as if He were washing it clean and ironing it out. Then to my great amazement, love welled up from my heart. I felt sympathy for the man I'd hated. I was so changed; I prayed sincerely that he might repent and come to God. Now I am afraid to look at this dagger. Please throw it away for me, Pastor.''

From that day she became a new person. She began to smile and eventually she married a fine man with whom she's happy. Though every man or woman forsake us, God does not! Though all others accuse us and treat us with contempt, God embraces us to His warm bosom. Though others do not trust in us, God trusts in us to the end. Though other people say, "This is the end," God says, "No, this is just the beginning." Though we regard ourselves as being less than the dust of the earth, God regards us as being greater than this universe.

33

Who then is God who loves us so much?

The Bible says that God is love (see 1 John 4:8). When we call God "our Father" we should remember that our Father is love. How much did He love us? God loved us enough to send His Son to hang on the cross until His flesh was torn and His blood was poured out. The prophet Isaiah describes the divine love beautifully: "But he was wounded for our transgression, he was bruised for our iniquities: the chastisement of our peace was upon him; and with his stripes we are healed. All we like sheep have gone astray; we have turned every one to his own way; and the Lord hath laid on him the iniquity of us all" (Is. 53:5,6).

Jesus was crucified as the expression of self-sacrificing, divine love. God does not take note of our position and circumstance. Romans 8:38,39 says, "For I am persuaded, that neither death, nor life, nor angels, nor principalities, nor powers, nor things present, nor things to come, nor height, nor depth, nor any other creature, shall be able to separate us from the love of God which is in Christ Jesus our Lord."

The depth of someone's love can be measured by the obstacles that person will overcome for us. God through His Son overcame the obstacle of death for us. Through one word God could have delivered thousands of heavenly hosts to release Jesus from the cross. But God the Father and the Son willingly agreed that Jesus would suffer and die for us. Jesus showed His solidarity with the Father in the Garden of Gethsemane when He prayed, "O my Father, if it be possible, let this cup pass from me; nevertheless not as I will, but as thou wilt" (Matt. 26:39).

The cup Jesus drank contained all our filthy sins. It was the bitter cup of judgment we and our children could not have avoided drinking if Jesus had not drunk it for us. Facing this cup Jesus expressed His pain: "My soul is exceeding sorrowful, even unto death" (Matt. 26:38).

God turned His face away from His only Son when He drank the cup and hung on the cross. He could not face the sin His Son carried when He cried, "My God, My God, why hast Thou forsaken me?"

Why did the Father and Son undergo the suffering to the end? Because God wanted to remove the obstacle that keeps us from knowing Him. This is the love of God our Father which conquered death.

No obstacle is too big or too high for God's love, not even principalities, for Jesus has the power of both heaven and earth in one hand. Not things present, nor things to come. Not powers. Not height nor depth, for Jesus descended into the deep and destroyed the power of death. He now sits at the right hand of the throne of God the Father. This is God's love.

When we are aware of His divine love, a wonderful change takes place. We find in ourselves a value higher than any other in the world. Because Jesus Christ, the most valued creature ever to walk this earth, died for us, we can say, "I am a most valuable person; Jesus died for me." When we make such a confession with boldness, there is nothing in this world to fear.

Many years ago, before I believed in Jesus, my family lived in a mountain village that had no water supply. We had to buy water from the waterbearers who carried buckets full of water on their shoulders. By the time they reached the top of that steep hill their faces were distorted with pain. One waterbearer, however, always had a pleasant smile on his face. I'd often noticed he'd even be singing. Whenever I saw him, a pleasant feeling came over me, and I always bought water from him.

One day I said, "You always sing a song when you bring the waterbuckets. What makes you so happy?"

He answered, "I am a Christian. God loves me and He is with me. Why shouldn't I be happy? You believe in Jesus, too!"

From all evidence, the waterbearer had nothing to make him happy, yet he was always full of joy. Later I came to understand the joy he had and I found out that the song he sang was the hymn "Nearer, My God, to Thee."

When we become the children of God and call God "our Father," we see, know and feel the immeasurable love of God. We are no more inferior persons, but superior persons.

Though we meet failures, we regard them as new opportunities instead of obstacles and defeats. We always see ourselves as overcomers, for God always triumphs; because we are His children, we will triumph also. The Bible says that God has no pleasure in us when we become disappointed and draw back (Heb. 10:38).

Though we may not have many worldly possessions and though we are only "common" people who don't have praiseworthy or honored qualities in the world's eyes, our inner beings are never ordinary. Each believer is a child of God who will inherit the kingdom of heaven; every one of us is a royal priest. Therefore those who can call God "Father" can and should live above and beyond any feelings of inferiority. When we come to our Father through Jesus and ask for victory, we will receive deliverance.

God Makes Us Rejoice

When we say, "Our Father which art in heaven," we can be assured that we aren't alone. There's nothing worse than feeling totally alone and abandoned. People can be walking down a teeming sidewalk yet feel isolated, yearning for someone to whom they can bare their hearts' needs, yearning for someone with whom they can have conversation. Prolonged loneliness can drive one into a blind alley until one finally explodes.

Several years ago when I was in the United States the local newspaper featured a story about a Korean college girl who threw herself from a tall building. She left a note that said death was her only escape from the insurmountable loneliness that engulfed her. She had worked hard to earn her school tuition. After a day's classes she had gone straight to a restaurant where she had washed dishes and scrubbed the floor. After that, she had babysat. Since English was her second language, she found communication difficult. She didn't see returning to Korea as an alternative—until she had earned her degree. And that goal seemed too far away. The loneliness became too much to bear, so she ended her life.

Loneliness is not a problem restricted to students who study in foreign countries. Loneliness haunts celebrities who have achieved success in their own fields, who receive respect and love from masses of people.

As I see it, the loneliest character in the Bible was Judas Iscariot. Several times through direct and indirect means Jesus admonished Judas Iscariot to turn around. But Judas made up his mind to sell Jesus. At the Last Supper he left the other disciples and went out into the darkness of a lonely night. In the end he was not only forsaken by God and the high priests; he even abandoned himself, giving up on life and hanging himself out of that severe loneliness.

How can anyone find his or her way out of loneliness? People usually resort to two methods. One is egoism. They try to live a totally egocentric life. Like the prodigal son, they always seek their own portion: my money, my honor, my power, my position, my men, my joy. Their pursuit really knows no end. But egoism is the short-cut that brings them back around to loneliness.

Today's world is so diffused with egoism that it can be noticed even in the family setting. The husband who always wants to be honored and loved is lonely even though he is with his wife and children. Children who regard their parents as mere guardians try to leave their home because they are lonely. Loneliness takes roots among friends, colleagues, teachers and students. The more egoistic one becomes, the higher the castle of loneliness becomes.

A second method people use to rid themselves of loneliness is to seek pleasure. They disregard proper relationships and pursue what pleases them.

That's what Eve did when she took the forbidden fruit that was "good for food" and "pleasant to the eyes" (Gen. 3:6). Since then humankind has lived according to its own will instead of the will of God.

The human mind is a divine gift. Through the unfallen mind Adam and Eve were able to obey the voice of God. As soon as dialogue with God was severed, reason became the authority by which one discerned good and evil. But reason alone is incomplete.

Reason is always manipulated by the flesh which is full of greed. Reason always provides an excuse—though not a reason—for any behavior that satisfies the flesh. The notion that men and women would be happy and good if they could only leave society for a life of wild freedom is simply not true.

Reason alone is not able to judge whether or not we are free. Such judgment is determined by lustful senses and these senses are always inclined toward pleasure.

Pleasure is like a pit that can never be filled. The more we give ourselves to pleasure, the deeper and wider the pit becomes. As pleasure is added to pleasure, our hearts become more and more lonely. Out of this loneliness people finally surrender their eternal freedom. Some are restrained by law for their crimes; some are sentenced to eternal destruction and fall to hell by means of suicide. Pleasure cannot liberate from loneliness.

How can we then be delivered from this alienation? There is only one way and that is when we call God "Father." Though everybody in the world forsakes us, our Father God does not forsake us. Although some earthly parents may desert the children they do not want or cannot care for, our Father doesn't forsake us. The Bible reads, "Do not err, my beloved brethren. Every good gift and every perfect gift is from above, and cometh down from the Father of lights, with whom is no variableness, neither shadow or turning. Of his own will begat he us with the word of truth, that we should be a kind of firstfruits of his creatures" (James 1:16-18). "For the gifts and calling of God are without repentance" (Rom. 11:29). "I will never leave thee, nor forsake thee" (Heb. 13:5).

The Holy Spirit is the Comforter who has been sent to help us. He is always with us. The Holy Spirit knows our infirmities and helps us. He knows even what we do not yet know and "maketh intercession for us with groanings which cannot be uttered" (Rom. 8:26).

The world neither sees nor knows nor receives the Holy Spirit, but we know Him and dwell with Him and realize that He is within us (see John 14:17).

When we pray aloud saying, "Our Father which art in heaven," loneliness and a sense of being forsaken depart from our hearts. We begin to seek a deeper meaning of life. We become freed from egoism. We do not look elsewhere to seek worldly joy. We try to become brothers and sisters and work to reduce the isolation in others' situations. We love our neighbors. If God becomes our Father, these are the wonderful things that will happen.

Hallowed Be Thy Name

What kind of life should we, as children of God, lead? Jesus teaches us that we should pray, "Hallowed be thy name." Children either become an honor to their parents or a shame to their parents, and Jesus charges us to live so that the name of God may be hallowed.

We can hallow God's name by serving and worshipping Him. The Bible says that God has made us priests, "But ye are a chosen generation, a royal priesthood, an holy nation, a peculiar people; that ye should shew forth the praises of him who hath called you out of darkness into his marvelous light" (1 Pet. 2:9).

If we have become priests, we should be offering sacrifices to God—sacrifices of thanksgiving, which honor God (Ps. 50:23). We should also offer praises. Hebrews 13:15,16 reads, "By him therefore let us offer the sacrifice of praise to God continually, that is, the fruit of our lips giving thanks to his name. But to do good and to communicate forget not: for with such sacrifices God is well pleased."

As we love others we offer a sacrifice in which the name of God is hallowed. Though Cornelius was a Gentile, he gave generously to those in need. As he prayed, an angel of God appeared to him and acknowledged that Cornelius's prayers and alms had come before God as a memorial (see Acts 10:4).

Likewise, we should sacrifice offerings of material things. Paul acknowledged this when he said, "But I have all, and abound: I am full, having received of Epaphroditus the things which were sent from you, an odour of a sweet smell, a sacrifice acceptable, well-pleasing to God" (Phil. 4:18).

Finally we honor our Father as we offer a living sacrifice. "I beseech you therefore, brethren, by the mercies of God, that ye present your bodies a living sacrifice, holy, acceptable unto God, which is your reasonable service'' (Rom. 12:1).

How can we present our bodies a living sacrifice? We should refrain from such things as drunkenness, lewdness, wantonness and licentiousness. Our body is the holy temple where God dwells (see 1 Cor. 3:16,17).

When we, as priests, live lives of sacrifice to our Father, He receives the glory and His heart rejoices. As a result of our obedience, His name is hallowed by others who see His work in our lives.

We also hallow God's name when we live with authority and use it. If we are calling God ''Father'' while we still fear the devil and are fettered by him, we are bringing shame to God.

If we have become children of God, we are free of bondage: ''Stand fast therefore in the liberty wherewith Christ hath made us free, and be not entangled again with the yoke of bondage'' (Gal. 5:1). ''Submit yourselves therefore to God. Resist the devil, and he will flee from you'' (James 4:7). Resisting the devil is the privilege of God's children—and their responsibility.

God is holy. Although we can by no means add anything to His holiness, it is our duty as children to give glory to our holy Father. We must make the world know the holiness of God through our worship services. But more, our lives should be a continual worship, offered to God day and night. Through our good words and deeds, the world will know the holiness of our Father. They will glorify the name of God when they see the authority we have to oppose and capture the devil.

Our Father which art in heaven, hallowed be Your holy and good name.

This is the key to our prayer. If our thoughts on God

41

are right, the other parts of our prayer will flow and be accomplished, like water running through a water pipe.

2

Thy Kingdom Come

The second prayer Jesus taught us is "Thy kingdom come. Thy will be done in earth, as it is in heaven." When God becomes our Father, we become the people of the kingdom of God. As such, we should pray that His kingdom stands firmly. What is the kingdom of God? It is the place where His sovereignty is accomplished.

As we consider these lines of prayer, let's align our thinking with God's words in relation to His kingdom and His will accomplished on this earth.

Our Created Earth: Fallen

Almost every day large headlines of horrible crimes splash across newspapers. Sometimes it's international

43

news. Sometimes it's the news from the city desk. Economic offenses inflict millions of dollars of damages. There are reports of brutal homicides, thieves in elevators, hit-and-run drivers, food contamination by agricultural chemicals, counterfeit merchandise. This daily reading makes you feel as if you are walking on thin ice. Recently a girl sent me a letter full of questions. "Why did God make such a world? Why does God remain indifferent about all of these things?"

I can assure you that the world God made in the beginning was not like this. Genesis describes a world that was totally different from the world of today. After God created heaven and earth (Gen. 1:1), Lucifer, who had been one of the cherubs of God, rebelled against Him intending to become as high as God. As a result, the world was judged and fell into chaos—void and filled with darkness (Gen. 1:2). Out of such chaos God re-created our present world in six days.

In your mind picture the process by which God created heaven and earth. On the first day, when God said, "Let there be light," bright light poured in like the morning when the spring rain is just over. On the second day, God created the boundless heaven. On the third day, the seas and the earth were divided distinctly. On the same day, the earth was covered with all kinds of plants.

On the next day, God created the sun and the moon and stars. And when God said, "Let the waters bring forth abundantly the moving creature that hath life, and fowl that may fly above the earth in the open firmament of heaven" (Gen. 1:20), the world was filled with all kinds of living creatures. On the sixth day, the last day of His creation, God created man and woman in His own image and gave them authority to rule over the world which God had created—a great and beautiful world where there was order instead of disorder, light instead of darkness, life instead of death, plenty instead of poverty, hope instead of despair. At that time the stronger did not prey upon the weaker.

The Garden of Eden which God planted for Adam and Eve was also an orderly and beautiful world, full of vitality and everything needed to satisfy all kinds of human needs. Even the fruit hanging on the branches of trees was pleasant to the sight and good for food.

Such was the world God created. Regrettably, however, such a world does not exist any more, for Adam and Eve were banished from the Garden of Eden because of their sin. As soon as Adam and Eve sinned, confusion, chaos, a violent temper and despair entered this world. Paul described what happened:

> And even as they did not like to retain God in their knowledge, God gave them over to a reprobate mind, to do those things which are not convenient; being filled with all unrighteousness, fornication, wickedness, covetousness, maliciousness; full of envy, murder, debate, deceit, malignity, whisperers, backbiters, haters of God, despiteful, proud, boasters, inventors of evil things, disobedient to parents, without understanding, covenantbreakers, without natural affection, implacable, unmerciful: who knowing the judgment of God, that they which commit such things are worthy of death, not only do the same, but have pleasure in them that do them (Rom. 1:28-32).

Why did these things happen? Mankind did not like to retain God in his knowledge. When God made man, He ran a big risk. Making man in His own likeness and image involved providing a free will—with which Adam and Eve were able either to accept or forsake God.

God wants to receive glory and worship. But He does not want us to worship Him mechanically like a puppet; that kind of worship is not offered in spirit and truth. Thanks and praise become hypocrisy unless they are given voluntarily.

Out of love God gave mankind a free will to worship Him. Those who love each other respect each other's personality. They don't force their own will on another.

When tempted by Satan, Adam and Eve refused to worship God and did not want Him in their hearts. Because of this underlying quality of free will, even God could not change man's choice. Men and women lost God and Satan took God's place in the human heart. Satan began to control their thoughts, words and deeds. Their willingness to disobey God reflected the desires of their hearts. Hence Satan's dominion over them was natural.

When Satan started his reign over this world, it turned into a wretched and tragic place. Satan comes to steal, kill and destroy (John 10:10). Satan comes to us and takes the divine image from us. He kills the spirit, soul and body that we may fall to destruction—eternal judgment and torment. Therefore, this world where we live with deep groaning came into being by mankind's chaos through Satan; it is not the world God created.

The Holy Spirit says clearly through the apostle Paul that this world will become more and more wicked in the last days.

This know also, that in the last days perilous times shall come. For men shall be lovers of their own selves, covetous, boasters, proud, blasphemers, disobedient to parents, unthankful, unholy, without natural affection, trucebreakers, false accusers, incontinent, fierce, despisers of those that are good, traitors, heady, highminded, lovers of pleasures more than lovers of God; having a form of godliness, but denying the power thereof: from such turn away (2 Tim. 3:1-5).

God who foreknows the future warns us to turn away from such an evil state of affairs. We are now seeing the destruction Satan has wreaked. But will this world remain forever under the rule of Satan? Is the world we see in the pages of the newspaper the final destiny of mankind?

The answer is no. Foreknowing the end result even before the fall of Adam and Eve, God predestined to set up the kingdom of hope—His kingdom where His sovereignty would be accomplished in this world of despair. He put on flesh and came to this world so His kingdom and divine will would be fulfilled upon this earth through Jesus.

The Kingdom of God

The kingdom of God is neither an institution nor a visible organization. However moral a state may be, it cannot become the kingdom of God. The kingdom of God is in a totally different realm; a spiritual realm where God manages, controls and governs the destiny of nations and individuals. God restores this world and retrieves us who were made in His image. It is a state where God becomes our Father and gives us all the blessings He prepares for us. It is a kingdom where we worship God, praise His holy name and make the requests of our hearts known to Him. Jesus taught His disciples that they should pray that the kingdom of God might come.

Jesus Taught the Kingdom

Jesus became man to bring the kingdom of God to this

earth. As the Allied forces landed on Normandy to free Europe from the occupation of Nazi Germany, so Jesus put on flesh and came to this world to free mankind from the rule of Satan. He came into this world where Satan was reigning so that He might build—accomplish and enlarge—His kingdom.

Jesus taught us many things about the kingdom of God. Let's look at five characteristics of the kingdom as found in His teachings and acts.

1. *The kingdom of God is a kingdom where there is no sin.* Jesus preached, "Repent: for the kingdom of heaven is at hand" (Matt. 4:17). Since God is righteous and holy, no one can enter the kingdom of heaven in a sinful state. The kingdom of God cannot come to an individual unless he is first forgiven of sins and justified before God. Jesus said that we must repent before our sins would be forgiven.

God still gives mankind the free will to choose. God constrains us to repent, but He does not threaten us. To the last moment, Jesus urged Judas Iscariot to repent. However Judas hardened his heart and went to ruin.

Jesus still commands us to repent that we may become citizens of the kingdom of heaven. Repentance is a definite decision to turn completely from one's sin and to obey the will of God. If we only make up our minds to repent, the Holy Spirit will bring to our remembrance all of the sins we have committed consciously or subconsciously and help us repent with our lips. The Bible says clearly, "I say unto you, that likewise joy shall be in heaven over one sinner that repenteth, more than over ninety and nine just persons, which need no repentance" (Luke 15:7).

The angels rejoice because the kingdom of heaven comes to that person who repents. We can't enter the kingdom of heaven unless we are cleansed from

48

wickedness, corruption, unrighteousness and confusion. Therefore, repentance is a prerequisite for the presence of the kingdom of God in an individual. And if we repent of our sins and receive forgiveness, we are no more tormented by a guilty conscience caused by Satan's greatest weapon, accusation.

2. *The kingdom Jesus brought to us is the kingdom of healing.* Matthew says,

> And Jesus went about all Galilee, teaching in their synagogues, and preaching the gospel of the kingdom, and healing all manner of sickness and all manner of disease among the people. And his fame went throughout all Syria: and they brought unto him all sick people that were taken with divers diseases and torments, and those which were lunatic, and those that had the palsy: and he healed them. And there followed him great multitudes of people from Galilee, and from Decapolis, and from Jerusalem, and from Judea, and from beyond Jordan (Matt. 4:23-25).

While preaching the good news of the kingdom of heaven, Jesus healed all manner of sick people as a sign and proof of the kingdom. Where did sickness come from? Death came as the wages of Adam and Eve's sin and mortality made mankind subject to sickness. Satan also caused mankind to be taken with mental sickness brought on by all kinds of diseases.

It was the will of God to forgive us for our sins and enable us to work for His kingdom with a sound body— delivered from diseases. Wherever the Word of God is preached and repentance is made, healing should follow.

While he was in prison, John the Baptist sent his disciples to Jesus to relay a question: ''Art thou he that should come, or do we look for another?'' (Matt. 11:3).

Of course John knew very well that the Son of God was to deliver men from sin. As the surest proof that He had come to set up the kingdom of God, Jesus answered, ''Go and shew John again those things which ye do hear and see: The blind receive their sight, and the lame walk, the lepers are cleansed, and the deaf hear, the dead are raised up, and the poor have the gospel preached to them'' (Matt. 11:4,5).

Jesus made it clear that healing was a sign of the coming of the kingdom of God to the earth.

3. *When Jesus preached the good news of the kingdom of heaven, unclean spirits departed.* Satan's evil spirits can never have a portion in the kingdom of heaven; they were driven out from the presence of God the day they rebelled against Him. Driven out of the kingdom of God, they had power of the air. When the Jewish leaders found fault with Jesus' casting out of the unclean spirits, He answered, ''But if I with the finger of God cast out devils, no doubt the kingdom of God is come upon you'' (Luke 11:20).

Jesus cast out evil spirits whenever He saw people oppressed. The devils simply could not stand His presence. When Jesus sent out His disciples to preach, He gave them authority to cast out demons (Luke 10:17-20), and Jesus also said that casting out devils would be a sign that would follow them that believe (Mark 16:17).

To this day, where the good news of the kingdom of heaven is preached, devils should be cast out in Jesus' name.

4. *In the kingdom of God there is no poverty.* Jesus had all wealth at His disposal. Heaven and earth and all things in them were created by Jesus' word; He was the Creator, yet He lived in such poverty that He didn't have a place to lay His body. Why did Jesus live in poverty?

The Bible says, "For ye know the grace of our Lord Jesus Christ, that though he was rich, yet for your sakes he became poor, that ye through his poverty might be rich" (2 Cor. 8:9). He became poor to make us rich.

Because of the sin of our first parents, Adam and Eve, mankind was cursed to live and eat bread by the sweat of the brow. A curse always followed those who did not keep the law. Because no one could keep the law, all fell under the curse (Deut. 28:16-19). But we are no more under the curse of the law because Jesus delivered us from the curse. Concerning that, Paul says, "Christ hath redeemed us from the curse of the law, being made a curse for us: for it is written, Cursed is every one that hangeth on a tree: that the blessing of Abraham might come on the Gentiles through Jesus Christ; that we might receive the promise of the Spirit through faith" (Gal. 3:13,14).

As long as we live in the kingdom of heaven we are poor people no more. We are the children of Abraham in faith. The blessings given to Abraham—the blessing of salvation in which he acquired the citizenship of the kingdom of heaven; the blessing of prosperity which made Abraham a rich man; the blessing of children and health—all these blessings come also to us. There is no poverty in the kingdom of heaven. Wherever the kingdom of heaven is proclaimed today, poverty should leave.

5. *The kingdom of heaven which Jesus brought to earth has opened the way for us to enter eternal life through faith.* "And as Moses lifted up the serpent in the wilderness, even so must the Son of man be lifted up: that whosoever believeth in him should not perish, but have eternal life" (John 3:14,15).

No one can be saved through his own righteous acts. There is no one who is qualified to come into God's presence on the merit of deeds. But regardless of sex, age and possession, whoever looks to Jesus, believes in Him as Savior and verbally confesses Him freely receives remission of sins and everlasting life. As Jesus said to the Samaritan woman, "And this is the will of him that sent me, that every one which seeth the Son, and believeth on him, may have everlasting life: and I will raise him up at the last day" (John 6:40).

In the kingdom of heaven there is eternal life. Those who become citizens of the kingdom receive this everlasting life, the life of God that is an assurance of salvation.

The Kingdom of Heaven Planted on Earth

Jesus not only taught us what the kingdom of God was; He was crucified to assure that the kingdom would last among us forever. By His crucifixion Jesus sowed seeds of the kingdom of God—eternal life, joy, hope and plenty—upon the kingdom of Satan, a land full of curses. "I am come to send fire on the earth; and what will I if it be already kindled?" (Luke 12:49).

The kingdom of God which we are eager to see come to this earth started to be established with the cross of Jesus. The kingdom of God has steadfastly been built upon the cross and the works of God. How did the cross start to establish God's kingdom on earth?

Jesus' death paid the price for our sin. While the sinless Jesus hung on the cross He willingly shed His blood, the only blood that had the power to remit the sins of all who would come to Him for repentance.

Second, Jesus carried our sickness by the wounds He bore. The Bible says that we are healed by the stripes of Jesus (1 Pet. 2:24).

Third, on the cross and with His resurrection, Jesus regained the right over this world which had gone to

Satan when Adam and Eve sinned.

In addition, by wearing the crown of thorns on Calvary, Jesus took away the curse of our poverty and gave us the right to receive blessings. And last, the blood of Jesus and His torn flesh became the way by which we are led to everlasting life.

Through His death and resurrection Jesus planted the kingdom of God upon this earth. When He returned to His Father, a successor came to expand this kingdom: the Holy Spirit.

> And when the day of Pentecost was fully come, they were all with one accord in one place. And suddenly there came a sound from heaven as of a rushing wind, and it filled all the house where they were sitting. And there appeared unto them cloven tongues like as of fire, and it sat upon each of them. And they were all filled with the Holy Ghost, and began to speak with other tongues, as the Spirit gave them utterance (Acts 2:1-4).

The Holy Spirit has come to help us and He is here today. He is nearby to take care of the heavenly seed which Jesus sowed. He is guaranteeing that it grows well and bears fruit. He comes and teaches us truth. He brings everything Jesus said to our remembrance and leads us into the right paths that we may live according to the Word.

So the Holy Spirit works for the expansion of the kingdom of God on earth. The Holy Spirit also works through us to increase the number of people in the kingdom. With the Holy Spirit in us we become the soldiers of faith waging a holy war the victory of which has already been assured. Through this righteous war, the kingdom of heaven is flourishing more and more.

Where then is the kingdom of heaven Jesus planted on earth?

The Kingdom of Heaven in Our Hearts

And when he was demanded of the Pharisees, when the kingdom of God should come, he answered them and said, The kingdom of God cometh not with observation: neither shall they say, Lo here! or, Lo there! for, behold, the kingdom of God is within you (Luke 17:20,21).

Jesus repeatedly preached the good news of the kingdom of heaven. His purpose was to teach the people what the kingdom is and to make them citizens of that kingdom. Then one day the Pharisees asked Him when the kingdom of God was going to come. They still had the false expectation that the kingdom of God would come to them in the form of a nation of this world. But Jesus said to them, "The kingdom of God is within you."

When we accept Jesus in our hearts as Savior and confess Him with our mouths, the Holy Spirit implants an assurance in our hearts. The Holy Spirit dwells in our bodies making us temples of God and from that moment on we are under the rule of God our Father. This inner place where God rules and reigns is the very place where the kingdom of God is set.

We are new creatures: "Therefore if any man be in Christ, he is a new creature: old things are passed away; behold, all things are become new" (2 Cor. 5:17). Several times Jesus compared the kingdom of God to the process by which seeds grow into plants. When the kingdom of heaven or the kingdom of God comes to our hearts, it begins to grow through our thoughts. Therefore our faith and thoughts should grow until they reach the faith and thoughts of God. Such a growth should continue until we meet Jesus face to face.

The Bible says, "Now unto him that is able to do exceeding abundantly above all that we ask or think, according to the power that worketh in us" (Eph. 3:20). If our thoughts reach the thoughts of God, we can see the hand of God accomplishing things. Every day we can live victorious lives destroying Satan; for God who is within us is greater than Satan who has the power of the air of the world (1 John 4:4).

So the kingdom of heaven exists in our hearts through Jesus and the power of the Holy Spirit. Though we live in a world full of chaos, emptiness and darkness, a new world has budded in our hearts. A new kingdom is come. The characteristics of the kingdom of God of which Jesus preached and which He planted on the cross are actually taking place in the midst of our lives. We are forgiven of our sins. We are healed. The demons are driven out from us. We are released from poverty. We are delivered from the curse and we have received everlasting life through faith.

When these things happen to our lives, we have proof that the kingdom of God is within us. Such signs will follow those who believe in Jesus and confess Him with their mouths.

But it is lamentable that many people just tread the precinct of the church, not knowing or understanding the new world which is in their hearts—nor do they try to believe in it. They don't know this grace and privilege—the new order and new power and the new world which comes when we call God "Father." "My people are destroyed for lack of knowledge" (Hos. 4:6). This saying of Hosea refers to such an occasion. Jesus also said to the Israelites who did not know the truth, "And ye shall know the truth, and the truth shall make you free" (John 8:32).

When people consider attending church, many merely choose the most convenient place to touch base with religion. They think that the church is the place to hear lessons of great men of the past, to cultivate their moral aspect of life or to find an ethical standard by which they can live.

Our faith in Christ is not a religion, however. It is neither culture nor morality. It is an experience with Jesus Christ! It is something new which happens in our hearts. It is an extraordinary event in which God, the Creator of heaven and earth, bought us with the sinless blood of Jesus Christ and planted His kingdom in us.

When we are the people of God, we no longer have to suffer the pangs of guilty conscience because of sin. We don't have to be oppressed by Satan any longer or be in bondage to him. Since the kingdom of God is within our hearts, it is our right to enjoy the privilege of the kingdom. The Bible exhorts us urgently, "Stand fast therefore in the liberty wherewith Christ hath made us free, and be not entangled again with the yoke of bondage" (Gal. 5:1). We no longer have to compromise with sin.

When you pray, "Thy kingdom come," remember that God takes possession of your heart. Remember also that this prayer calls for complete dedication of your heart to God. This prayer is the pronouncement of your faith in and obedience to God the Father. Through this prayer you receive the commission to preach the kingdom of God come. The most effective way to carry out this commission is to enjoy the privilege of the kingdom and live in it daily.

Praying That God's Will Be Done

It is not enough that the kingdom of God is within us. The kingdom of God should be fulfilled and be evident in the life, family and environment of the citizens of that kingdom.

God wills that mankind be redeemed. He wants to deliver mankind from the threefold fall (of the spirit, soul and body) by the threefold work of Jesus: His crucifixion, death and resurrection. Before the foundation of the world, God had purposed this with Jesus and throughout history He had shown His promise to mankind till finally Jesus came to this earth—conceived in the body of the virgin Mary.

When this happened, the divine will was already known to the angels of heaven and the prophets of the Lord. When this divine will was fulfilled, the hosts of heaven sang, "Glory to God in the highest, and on earth peace, good will toward men" (Luke 2:14). This divine will, which was fulfilled through Jesus' coming to this world, brought glory to God and peace to this world.

What is the right attitude we should have as we pray that God's will—to redeem and forgive mankind and to bless people in soul, body and environment—be done on earth?

We should think as God does: positively, creatively and redemptively. From beginning to end the Bible, the divine revelation through human writings, is full of such thought patterns. Some Scripture verses may seem stupid to our human thinking. Yet the Bible says, "The foolishness of God is wiser than men" (1 Cor. 1:25).

In our minds we can set in motion the work of the kingdom. On the canvas of our minds we can paint pictures of things that don't exist. As Proverbs says, "Where there is no vision, the people perish" (29:18). We can be envisioners of the divine will done on earth. "I will pour out my spirit upon all flesh: and your sons and your daughters shall prophesy, and your young men shall see visions, and your old men shall dream dreams" (Acts 2:17).

After we start thinking positively, creatively and redemptively, we should have dreams of what we can become in Christ. Those who are sick among us should have dreams of good health. Those who are poor should dream of having plenty; those in discordant families should dream of seeing peace and harmony in our dreams and visions, by the power of the Holy Spirit they will actually come into reality; such "dreams" are born in our hearts by the Holy Spirit.

Based on Hebrews 11:3, "...things which are seen were not made of things which do appear," we should *see* things which are not visible; we should *consider* things which are not visible; we should *dream* pictures of situations which are not visible. One who cannot cherish clearbright dreams of tomorrow in his or her heart cannot create anything; through such a person God's divine will cannot be done in this earth.

Once we have drawn on the canvas of our mind things which are not visible, we should kneel down before God and pray in faith until we have the assurance that our dreams will come true. We should fast and pray, crying, "Oh God, let this dream of my heart be fulfilled through the power of the kingdom of God. Destroy all the hindrances of Satan." When we cry out to God and pray, fear and worry will soon disappear and supernatural faith will enter with overflowing assurance.

Hebrews 11:1 reads, "Faith is the substance of things hoped for, the evidence of things not seen." The Greek word for *substance* has two meanings: "a footboard" or "an underpinning" and "a deed." Faith is a support of what we hope and desire. Unless an underpinning is strong enough, we can't put anything on it. This underpinning comes through the assurance of our hearts when we pray. Substance is also like a land or house deed that certifies ownership. When we pray fervently with a burning desire and a clear-cut goal, assurance and peace of mind come to us that God's answer is on the way.

But the key step in having the will of God done in our lives is thanksgiving. God said that He would show His hand of salvation to those who offered the sacrifice of thanksgiving and praise. Seeds of faith are sown in thanksgiving.

Last, to see God's will being done on earth, we should expect a miracle. There will be times when we have to go through deep waters or when we have to pass through a fiery test. There will also be times when expecting a miracle involves climbing a mountain. But we always must take that first step. Even the Holy Spirit cannot work unless we start walking in faith. As we do, the Holy Spirit will be with us and we will finally win the victory. People around us will see the wonderful fulfillment of God's divine will and they will give glory to God. As you align your thoughts about the kingdom and will of God with Jesus' thoughts, as you step out in faith to reach the dreams God has set in your heart, the kingdom of God will reign—beginning in your heart, then in your family and then in your neighbor. And someday the eternal new heaven and new earth which are prepared for you will come in the brightness of glory.

3

Give Us This Day

When Jesus taught His disciples how to pray, He set things in proper order. He said that they—and we—should first call our good God "our Father." He said that we should pray that God's name be hallowed, that the kingdom of God's sovereign power should come and that His good will be done in earth. When our posture and relationship toward God become right in this way, our next prayer is for blessings, for daily bread. If we are not in the right relationship with God—if we can neither call God "Father" nor believe that He is our Father—it is useless to ask for our daily bread.

The problems of greatest concern to human beings are related to food, clothing and shelter. The ultimate goal of all political ideologies is to solve these problems. What do you think the mind of God is about these basic needs?

The mind of God is to give us our daily bread—a term that is broader than loaves made of flour. It includes all the necessary things that go with earning a living. In order to earn daily bread, one must have a job. To get a job, one must receive necessary training. One also needs a house for rest and commodities necessary to daily life.

Praying for our daily bread applies to all requests for necessities. Our Father God wants to fill all these needs.

What is the right thinking we must have as we ask for our daily bread? As we tune in to the mind of God, this prayer which Jesus taught us to say will be answered.

God Is Concerned With the Physical World

Today many people say that God does not concern Himself with material things. Some even assert that we should ask for spiritual things but not for our material needs to be met.

But is God indifferent to the physical world? The answer is definitely no. God prepared the physical world even before He created man and woman so that Adam and Eve did not have to worry about what they would eat, what they would put on or what they would drink.

When I was conducting a revival meeting in a small town in England, I accepted an invitation to a home where I rested and then ate dinner. As soon as I sat down to eat, the hostess shared her story. Through tears she said, "Pastor Cho, there is a reason I have invited you to my home. We have a big problem. Despite a painful effort to make a good living, we have failed in every business we have tried, and now we have a huge debt. Though we've prayed hard, there is no answer. We've lost our appetite from worry; we can't sleep soundly. Why are we getting into debt in spite of our hard effort to make a good living? What is the matter? We've even put our home up for sale. We intended to pay the debt by selling our house, but there haven't been interested buyers—even though it's been on the market for quite a while. Things are getting worse and worse every day."

As I listened to her story, I could easily see why she was not receiving God's blessings. From the beginning to the end of her conversation, the words she spoke were full of grudges, complaints and sighs. She spoke with unbelief; there were no words of positive and creative faith.

She knew little about God the Father. Instead of standing in faith on the Word of God, she was relying on her senses. When the circumstances were good, she was happy; when the circumstances became unfavorable, she became unhappy. She had not reached the faith that could change her destiny, that could create a new environment with an aggressive and positive spirit. She didn't have hope that stood firm even when she had no evidence of help. I said to her, "Sister, let us study the Bible until your husband comes home."

At my request she read Genesis 1:2-4: " 'And the earth was without form, and void; and darkness was upon the face of the deep. And the Spirit of God moved upon the face of the waters. And God said, Let there be light: and there was light. And God saw the light, that it was good.' "

"Sister," I said, "doesn't the Scripture sound a little strange?"

"No," she countered.

"Don't you think it was too much for God to create light alone—without the help of Adam and Eve? Wasn't it too much for Him?"

Very seriously, the woman read the words again. "The English Bible does not say that. Does the Korean Bible?"

"No, but isn't it somewhat strange—that God made light without the help of Adam and Eve? On the next day maybe God asked for their help. Go ahead, read further, verses six to eight."

" 'And God said, Let there be a firmament in the midst of the waters, and let it divide the waters from the waters. And God made the firmament, and divided the waters which were under the firmament from the waters which were above the firmament: and it was so. And God called the firmament Heaven.' "

I confirmed my questions. "Well, is there any mention that Adam helped God here?"

"No."

"But on the third day God may have needed help from Adam and Eve. Please keep going."

She continued, " 'And God said, Let the waters under the heaven be gathered together unto one place, and let the dry land appear: and it was so. And God called the dry land Earth; and the gathering together of the waters called he Seas...And God said, Let the earth bring forth grass, the herb yielding seed, and the fruit tree yielding fruit after his kind, whose seed is in itself, upon the earth: and it was so. And the earth brought forth grass, and herb yielding seed after his kind, and the tree yielding fruit, whose seed was in itself, after his kind.' "

"Did God ask for help from Adam and Eve?" I asked again.

"No, He didn't."

"Maybe on the fourth day God became tired...What happened next?"

"God created the sun, the moon and the stars."

"With any help from Adam or Eve?"

"No."

"How about on the fifth day?"

"No, God didn't need their help then either."

"On the sixth day?"

The woman read the passage closely and said, "Pastor, on the sixth day He made all the animals and then He made Adam and Eve—in His image and after His likeness. So no, God didn't need their help then."

"Really? What about the seventh day?"

"God rested from all His work."

"Was there any work for Adam and Eve to do the first day after they were created?"

"No, it doesn't seem so," she answered after pondering awhile.

I continued, "Before Adam and Eve greeted their first day—which really was the seventh day—God had made everything. The firmament and sun. The earth and every kind of fruit tree and vegetable. The sun, the moon and the stars. The birds of the air, the fish in the water and the animals on the earth. Since God had prepared everything for Adam and Eve, there was nothing they needed to provide. So what was required of them? If Adam and Eve had come to God and asked, 'Father, this is our first day on the earth. What task should we do?' What do you think God would have answered?"

"Well, God may have said, 'I have prepared everything for you. So don't worry over anything. Just live in faith and obedience.' "

"Exactly," I commented. "Since God had made heaven and earth and everything in the earth, there was nothing left for them to do. Through faith and obedience they could rest on God's Sabbath and enjoy everything God had prepared for them. All they had to do was just believe, have fellowship with God and live in obedience to Him—not worrying over anything."

"But because Adam and Eve refused to believe and obey God, because they tried to manage the world as they wished, the world has become as it is today. Yet even now, if we accept Jesus as Savior and come to God, He allows us to enjoy all things that Adam and Eve enjoyed before they rebelled against Him. According to the will of God, everything was accomplished through the cross of Jesus Christ. What we Christians should do is to believe, obey and enjoy. The Bible never says that Christians should make their living. It says that God has prepared everything for us.

"Now take a look at your own situation. As the result of your effort to prepare everything for your living, you have put aside God. Jeremiah 33:3 says, 'Call unto me, and I will answer thee, and shew thee great and mighty things, which thou knowest not.' All your problems—what to put on, what to eat and what to drink, even the problem of selling your house—are God's job. When you tried to solve them all by yourself, God took His hands off. But if you repent of your sin of disbelief, entrust everything to the Lord and walk in faith, obedience and thanks—expecting miracles to happen—the Lord will allow you to enjoy everything He has prepared."

The woman had listened intently, and hope revived in her heart. She said, "Pastor, no one has ever taught me this." Tears again came to her eyes, and I suggested that we pray together.

When we knelt I said, "Lord, I entrust her life to You. I leave everything to Your care and from this moment I take rest. I give thanks to You in faith and obedience. So let her house be sold and solve all her problems."

The following day I left that town to conduct revival meetings in another city. But soon I received a letter from this woman which said, "After you left our home, a wonderful thing happened to us. I repeated your sermon on Genesis to my husband. We repented of our faults in tears and gave the prayer of thanksgiving to God. After several days a couple looked at our house and offered to buy it—just the house they were looking for—at a price far higher than we had asked. We are going to move to a smaller but elegant and beautiful home. I have shared what you taught me with everyone I've met.''

Nature tells us of the plentifulness of God. Gardeners say that an apple tree needs thirty to fifty leaves to bear an apple. Yet a full-grown apple tree has more than 100,000 leaves—far more than are needed to bear fruit. Why does God give so many leaves to a fruit tree? Because God foresaw that worms would eat away leaves. He knew that storms would come and sweep away some leaves. He knew that some leaves would wither away because of drought. Because the plenteous God knew all these things beforehand, He provided extra leaves to prepare the apple tree for possible problems.

There are other natural examples: Female pheasants and quails, which nest on the ground, lay ten to thirty eggs—more than enough to preserve their species. But this guarantees the birds against weasels and skunks which steal eggs from the nests.

Such a God of plenty also provided Adam and Eve with everything, including the Garden of Eden. This God becomes our Father and commands us to ask that He give us everything He has prepared for us. Let this thought be firmly in you: Unless you have the image of the plentifulness of God, your prayer for daily bread will not have the faith to come up before God.

Has God actually shown Himself as the God of plentifulness in history? The answer is yes, as shown repeatedly in the Bible.

God Does Provide

In the Old Testament, some three million Israelites experienced the God of plenty during their forty-year

67

journey from Egypt to the land of Canaan. The wilderness did not naturally provide enough water or food to sustain the three million people. But every morning God gave them manna—just enough for the day at hand. God also brought forth water out of a rock, and He fed the Israelites with fresh meat by sending quails down to the camp in a great wind. Deuteronomy 8:4 describes another provision of God to His wandering people: "Thy raiment waxed not old upon thee, neither did thy foot swell, these forty years."

The land God promised to the children of Israel was frequently called "the land flowing with milk and honey." God still promises us that He will give His children "the land flowing with milk and honey" and He is actually fulfilling His promise today. God gives us our daily bread as abundantly as milk and honey flow. God is our Father today!

The miracles Jesus performed also prove that God provides daily bread. One day 5,000 men were listening to Jesus preach. As evening drew near, the crowd grew hungry. In that wilderness setting it was impossible to feed so many people by human means. But our Lord prepared "milk and honey" through a miracle. When He blessed five small barley loaves and two fishes and distributed them to the people, the food multiplied in amazing proportions. When the disciples cleaned up the fragments that remained, they collected twelve baskets full of leftovers (Matt. 14:16-21).

Such a thing did not happen only once, and a second biblical account always reinforces God's point. Matthew 15:32-38 records a similar incident in which Jesus fed 4,000 men (tens of thousands if the women and children had been included in the count) with seven loaves of bread and two fishes. Seven baskets of leftovers were collected. God does provide in accordance with our need.

The concern of Jesus for people's physical needs was also shown through His participation in Peter's catch of fish. Peter had been greatly disappointed that he had worked all night without catching a fish. Indeed it isn't a small thing when a fisherman can't catch a single fish. Apply that to the situation of your own life. Suppose you could not make a single dollar though you had worked a whole day. How disappointed and frustrated you would be. At that time Jesus said to Peter, "Launch out into the deep, and let down your nets for a draught" (Luke 5:4).

True to Jesus' word—draught—Peter hauled in such a great catch that his net broke. Peter's previous failure to catch any fish had nothing to do with his experience or inexperience. In the same way, our great expertise does not always ensure us our daily bread. Countless defeated people live in despair not knowing why they have failed. As Jesus came into Peter's boat and told him where to let down his net (Jesus helped Peter catch fish a second time, after Jesus' resurrection), so He wants to come into the center of our lives and miraculously provide our daily bread.

Jesus—God the Son who has prepared everything we need—not only told us to ask for our daily bread, but He showed us through examples that He can actually give us all we need. There is no reason why we should doubt that our prayers will be answered.

So far, the biblical examples I've cited have had to do with food. But the Bible also says that God wants to give us material things. Let's look at such scriptures:

But thou shalt remember the Lord thy God: for it is he that giveth thee power to get wealth, that he may establish his covenant which he sware unto thy fathers, as it is this day (Deut. 8:18).

69

And it shall come to pass, if thou shalt hearken diligently unto the voice of the Lord thy God, to observe and to do all his commandments which I command thee this day, that the Lord thy God will set thee on high above all nations of the earth: and all these blessings shall come on thee, and overtake thee, if thou shalt hearken unto the voice of the Lord thy God. Blessed shalt thou be in the city, and blessed shalt thou be in the field. Blessed shalt be the fruit of thy body, and the fruit of thy cattle, the increase of thy kine, and the flocks of thy sheep. Blessed shall be thy basket and thy store. Blessed shalt thou be when thou comest in; and blessed shalt thou be when thou goest out (Deut. 28:1-6).

Honour the Lord with thy substance, and with the firstfruits of all thine increase: so shall thy barns be filled with plenty, and thy presses shall burst out with new wine (Prov. 3:9-10).

O fear the Lord, ye his saints: for there is no want to them that fear him. The young lions do lack, and suffer hunger: but they that seek the Lord shall not want any good thing (Ps. 34:9-10).

These passages are only a few examples that indicate God's willingness to bless us with material things. But it is not enough to know and quote these scriptures. We must pray as Jesus taught us to pray as well as believe His Word.

Praying for Daily Needs

What attitudes should we set in our minds as we ask for our daily bread?

First, we should make a clear distinction between what

we should ask first and what we should ask later. Because mankind sometimes reversed the proper order, asking first what should have been asked later and asking later what should have been asked first, everything went wrong. The Bible reads, "And he humbled thee, and suffered thee to hunger, and fed thee with manna, which thou knewest not, neither did thy fathers know; that he might make thee know that man doth not live by bread only, but by every word that proceedeth out of the mouth of the Lord doth man live" (Deut. 8:3).

God sometimes permits us to go through paths of hardship and hunger to teach us a lesson: that we do not live by bread only. Our souls and spiritual needs must be top priority. When we receive and live in the Word of God, God will loose the material things He has prepared for us. This is what Jesus meant when He said, "But seek ye first the kingdom of God, and his righteousness; and all these things shall be added unto you" (Matt. 6:33).

Serving God must be our main job. If our main job prospers, all our side jobs are bound to succeed. When we take the side jobs as our main job, God teaches us with whips of punishment in order to put us back on the right track. Therefore, when we pray for our daily necessities, we should pray with a proper priority, putting first things first and last things last.

Second, we should show evidence that we do not serve gold as an idol. How can we show evidence that we don't love money more than God? By obeying God's commandment to pay our tithes.

> Bring ye all the tithes into the storehouse, that there may be meat in mine house, and prove me now herewith, saith the Lord of hosts, if I will not open you the windows of heaven, and pour you out a blessing, that there shall not be room enough to

receive it. And I will rebuke the devourer for your sakes, and he shall not destroy the fruits of your ground; neither shall your vine cast her fruit before the time in the field, saith the Lord of hosts (Mal. 3:10,11).

The tithe is not ours, but God's. We cannot dispose of it as we please. Malachi says that we should bring all the tithes into the storehouse of God. A lot of people do not do this because covetousness has darkened their eyes. By their disobedience they obstruct the power of God to loose the things He has prepared for them. When we bring all the tithes into God's storehouse, God blesses our barns and fills them with plenty.

Third, we must believe and confess our conviction that God will give to us abundantly. David forthrightly expressed his belief that God would provide: "The Lord is my shepherd; I shall not want. He maketh me to lie down in green pastures: he leadeth me beside the still waters" (Ps. 23:1,2). And Paul said, "But my God shall supply all your need according to his riches in glory by Christ Jesus" (Phil. 4:19). Many believers do not enjoy the abundance of God because they do not verbalize their belief that God abundantly gives good things to His children.

Finally, we must give thanks always—when we ask and when we receive. "Be careful for nothing; but in every thing by prayer and supplication with thanksgiving let your requests be made known unto God" (Phil. 4:6). How can we help but thank God for the sunlight, air, water, health and life we enjoy? Our thanksgiving and praise are the sweet fragrance of a sacrificial offering burning before God; it opens the way to His power and salvation.

Our God is the giver of sunlight, rain and all manner

of vegetation. It is natural for Him to give His children who obey Him in faith the land of Canaan flowing with milk and honey. Therefore we can pray boldly that God give us our daily bread. Beloved people of God, the God who saved you and poured out the Holy Spirit for you also wants to give you daily bread; He has prepared your daily bread.

Love the Lord your God with all your heart, with all your soul, with all your mind. Seek first His kingdom and righteousness. Pray for your daily bread in the name of Jesus. Then God will supply your needs as He gave manna to the children of Israel. He will. You don't need to worry.

4

Forgive Us Our Debts

We who have become children of God by the sinless blood of Jesus Christ now should pray to Him to forgive our sins. When the kingdom of God comes into our hearts and His will is present in our lives, God's forgiving grace and power should naturally come upon us. In the prayer Jesus taught His disciples—and us—He said that we should ask boldly and with assurance for our daily bread, for forgiveness of sins and for protection from temptation or evil.

As previously stated, we are to pray in line with the mind of God. And what is the mind of God concerning sin?

We Are Sinners and Deserve Death

The Greek word for *sin* means "missing the mark"— as an arrow might miss the target at which it was aimed. In order to give glory to God and please Him, man and woman should have lived in obedience and faith. This was the mark or target of human life.

Deceived by Satan, however, Adam and Eve took and ate the fruit of knowledge. They violated the commandment God had given to them: "But of the tree of the knowledge of good and evil, thou shalt not eat of it: for in the day that thou eatest thereof thou shalt surely die" (Gen. 2:17). As the willful expression of their disobedience and unbelief, this action meant that their behavior missed the mark of life and was sin before God. As a result, Adam and Eve felt shame and guilt. Satan gained the legitimate right to accuse, rule and rob mankind. "He that committeth sin is of the devil; for the devil sinneth from the beginning" (1 John 3:8).

Adam and Eve, with all their posterity, fell into the slavery of Satan. Sin entered the human world by the offense of one man, Adam, and all became sinners. "Wherefore, as by one man sin entered into the world, and death by sin; and so death passed upon all men, for that all have sinned" (Rom. 5:12). As the consequence of sin, they had to die. "For the wages of sin is death" (Rom. 6:23). The Greek word for *death* is *thanatos* which means "to be separated." As soon as death entered the human society through sin, man's dialogue with God was severed. As soon as man was separated from God, the source of life, man died. As soon as he was separated from the other creatures he had ruled, everything went wrong; as soon as God's hand of protection departed, diseases entered the human body. Furthermore, the unquenchable fire of hell is waiting to punish eternally all

76

who have not returned to Jesus to ask for and receive forgiveness for their sins.

Since men and women, created in the image of God, are spiritual beings, they are eager to be delivered from sin and death. But without fully paying the wages of sin, no one can get out of Satan's rule; no one can free himself from ultimate death. Because there is no one in the world who doesn't commit sin, it is foolish to expect anyone else in this world to be an effective Savior.

The human race needed someone who would help us, someone who would solve the problem of death. He could not be born of the seed of Adam, yet He had to be human—not angelic—for He had to atone for the sin of man. Though He had to be sinless, He was to be a human—one of us with ears, eyes, a mouth and a nose. Moreover He had to be someone who was willing to take the wages of our sin upon Himself and pay our redemption price on our behalf. In the human point of view this was absolutely impossible. Nevertheless, man had to be delivered from sin and death by such a Redeemer.

Such an impossible mission had to be accomplished. All the desires and hopes, the sighs and longings, of man since the creation can be boiled down to one phrase— deliverance from sin and the devil. Did the cry disappear into thin air like a sound without an echo? No. It reached the throne of God and the divine plan of God was fulfilled. Jesus Christ has come to save humankind.

The Divine Answer: Jesus Christ

God ordained that His sinless Son, Jesus Christ, should put on the form of human flesh and die instead of man. "For God so loved the world, that he gave his only begotten Son, that whosoever believeth in Him should not perish, but have everlasting life" (John 3:16).

77

By the will of God, Jesus Christ was born in this world of the virgin Mary in a manger in Bethlehem 2,000 years ago.

As the Bible says, the seed of the woman shall bruise the seed of the serpent (Gen. 3:15). Jesus was conceived of the seed of a woman but without a natural father. Fathered by the Holy Spirit, Jesus was not the seed of man but possessed sinless blood.

Jesus became flesh to be the sacrifice to atone for the sins of mankind. For this reason John the Baptist cried at the Jordan River, "Behold the Lamb of God, which taketh away the sin of the world" (John 1:29). Romans 4:25 also says that Jesus "was delivered for our offenses, and was raised again for our justification."

For our sake and in our place Jesus took upon His own body all the sins, wickedness, ugliness, curse and despair of the world.

High between heaven and earth He hung—with His hands and feet nailed to that cross, His head pierced by the crown of thorns and His side pierced by a spear. Through all these sufferings Jesus forever blotted out all our sins before God.

Since God has answered our wishes by sending His Son and has prepared the way through which we can be delivered from sin and death, we need only accept the redemption God has provided. We need to accept Jesus Christ, the Son of the living God, as our own personal Savior. Though God gave His Son for us, He cannot make us accept His Son as our Savior. As it was in the Garden of Eden, so now each person must decide and confess that decision verbally. The person who believes and confesses is delivered from the power of death; the person who does not accept through faith is still under the power of death.

Since God forgave our sins through Jesus Christ, our

problem of sin has been solved. If we go to hell, it is only because we do not accept the forgiveness God has offered.

When Andrew Jackson was the U.S. president, a man named George Wilson spotted a thief stealing something from a post office. Wilson shot the man to death and was arrested, convicted and sentenced to die. But because of the circumstances of the crime, President Jackson signed a special pardon which acquitted and discharged Wilson. Here the story becomes unusual. Wilson refused to accept the pardon, and a legal quandary ensued. This case was eventually appealed to the Supreme Court where John Marshall, the chief judge, gave a famous decision as follows: "The letter of pardon is merely a piece of paper, but it has the power to pardon as long as the person who is the object of pardon accepts it. If the person who is the object of pardon refused to accept it, he cannot be acquitted. Therefore the death penalty sentenced to George Wilson should be carried out."

George Wilson was certainly pardoned, but because he refused to accept his pardon, he was executed.

Our situation is just like that. God has pardoned the sins of mankind. Today the Holy Spirit of God is proclaiming to all: "Your sins are forgiven but you must come to Jesus and accept your pardon." The divine pardon has been given, but numerous people are not accepting it. There is no help for those who refuse to accept the pardon; they will face execution and have no one to blame but themselves.

When Jesus pardoned our sins, He did not forgive those only of the past nor only of the present. He atoned for all the sins of our lifetime—including the future—once and for all.

According to Hebrews 10:14-18,

For by one offering he hath perfected for ever them that are sanctified. Whereof the Holy Ghost also is a witness to us: for after that he had said before, This is the covenant that I will make with them after those days, saith the Lord, I will put my laws into their hearts, and in their minds will I write them; and their sins and iniquities will I remember no more. Now where remission of these is, there is no more offering for sin.

Because our Lord atoned for your sins and mine once and for all by one offering, we no longer need to offer sacrifice for our sins. Our sins have been written off; we are acquitted and discharged. If you believe in Jesus as your Savior and accept the forgiveness of God, you will be justified before God. You will be acknowledged as a person who has never sinned and you will have the privilege to stand before God. Satan will not be able to accuse you before the throne of God because your sins are under the blood of Jesus.

As We Forgive Our Debtors

To enjoy the forgiveness God has given us there is a condition we must meet. God gives us the grace of forgiveness continually when we forgive other people.

If we harbor hatred in our hearts and refuse to forgive people who have wronged us, the forgiveness we have already received will not be affected. But from that time on forgiveness needed for further faults will be cancelled. Jesus gave a parable of two debtors. One owed the king 10,000 talents and the other owed the first debtor 100 pence. The king forgave the debt of the man who owed him the large sum. But that man turned around and had no mercy toward the man who owed him a small amount. When the king found out what had happened, he was furious and punished the evil man. Here Jesus taught us the lesson that we should forgive the faults and wrongdoings of other people in the manner in which we have been forgiven. He said, "So likewise shall my heavenly Father do also unto you, if ye from your hearts forgive not everyone his brother their trespasses" (Matt. 18:35).

There is a direct link between the way we forgive our enemies and the way we will be forgiven. When Cain killed his brother Abel, God asked, "Where is Abel thy brother?" What did Cain say? "Am I my brother's keeper?" (Gen. 4:9). But we are the keepers of our brothers. God made humans as social beings. The book of Genesis says, "It is not good that the man should be alone; I will make him an help meet for him....Therefore shall a man leave his father and his mother, and shall cleave unto his wife: and they shall be one flesh" (2:18,24).

Since the creation of woman man has lived with other humans. We are destined to live together as couples, as parents with children, among neighbors. As long as anyone lives in community, he or she cannot ask such an irresponsible question as "Am I my brother's keeper?" For this reason Jesus taught us to pray, "Our Father..." instead of "My Father."

When people live together, sin inevitably enters their relationships. No one is perfect. Everyone has negative personality and character traits—ego, pride, jealousy, ambition. Wherever people get together, differences in character and personality become obvious and cause tension and pain. As time goes by, remorse over the past becomes present-tense hatred, and that is how this world has become full of envy, jealousy, calamity and murder. "But the wicked are like the troubled sea, when it cannot rest, whose waters cast up mire and dirt. There is no peace, saith my God, to the wicked" (Is. 57:20,21).

How can we live in peace and harmony with other people, forget old grudges and accept God's healing? With the progress of knowledge, we have invented all kinds of conveniences. But there is one field that has seen no progress at all: the field of social skill. Despite our communal destiny, man seems intent on making weapons that injure and kill others.

There is no one who can solve this problem of enmity and hate but Jesus Christ. He has forgiven us and insists that we pray, "Forgive us our debts, as we forgive our debtors." It's interesting that immediately after the ending of this prayer which Jesus taught His disciples, He returns to this topic of forgiveness. Matthew 6:14,15 goes on to say, "For if ye forgive men their trespasses, your heavenly Father will also forgive you: but if ye forgive not men their trespasses, neither will your Father forgive your trespasses."

One day John Wesley met one of his friends on the street. They hadn't met in some time and Wesley said, "I heard that you and Mr. So-and-So had become enemies. Have you come to terms with him?"

"No, I haven't," the man answered. "Why should I? He's the one who should be blamed. I'll never forgive him, for I am the one who was hurt."

Looking straight in the man's face, Wesley said, "Then you should never again commit sin. I don't think you can say you have never committed a sin. You have so far because somebody has forgiven your faults. But if you say that you don't want to forgive someone who has wronged you, from now on don't expect to be forgiven by anybody else either."

At this, the man dropped his head and repented bitterly of his faults.

If we don't want to forgive the faults of our neighbors, we should not commit sins. The husband who does not want to forgive the faults of his wife should not commit a fault himself. The wife who does not want to forgive the faults of her husband should not commit any faults either. If they do not forgive each other, their own fault cannot be forgiven.

All people heal each other by forgiving each other. No one is so righteous that he or she does not need to be forgiven. The warm outstretched hands of forgiveness start healing wounds almost immediately. We should never forget that we owe our righteousness to the forgiveness we have received from God; our debts are paid as we forgive the sins or debts which others owe us. The forgiveness of God comes when we forgive the offenses others have committed against us.

Because God has forgiven us, we owe the debt of forgiveness to others. The apostle Paul said, "I am debtor both to the Greeks, and to the Barbarians; both to the wise, and to the unwise" (Rom. 1:14). If a man like the apostle Paul was a debtor, then ordinary people like you and me are debtors who owe more. As much as I am forgiven, I should also forgive others day by day. We should do our best to pay the debt of forgiveness in our lifetime.

The Cost of Forgiveness

Forgiveness brings beautiful results. Where there is forgiveness, there is heaven—for the God of forgiveness is there through the Holy Spirit. Is it easy for anyone to forgive by sheer willpower? Those who have sincerely forgiven the faults and mistakes of others would certainly answer no. How does one forgive?

Forgiveness always demands a price—suffering—a

cross. Never believe that God's forgiveness to you and me did not cost God anything. It cost Him the sacrificial suffering of His only Son. Though we were the ones who sinned, Jesus had to take the sins upon Himself. The forgiver—not the forgiven—paid the price. Likewise, if we are to forgive others, it will cost us suffering and a cross. Why? It is not possible for us to forgive others while we are still insisting on our opinions, our rights, our bigotry. As we crucify our own pride, anger and thoughts, we will be able to forgive fully—with our heart as well as with our mouth. To forgive others, we must first die to self. Until that happens, hatred, pride, ill feelings and resentments will rise up continually, blocking our ability to forgive. We are delivered from ego-centeredness when we forgive. And we are set free from our obstinacy, arrogance and self-assertions; we enter into the true freedom of God.

Corrie ten Boom, who spent the last years of her life in the United States, was a famous Dutch revivalist. During World War II she and her family were arrested and transported to Nazi concentration camps on the charge that they hid Jews in their home. Her father and sister died in the camps, and Corrie returned home alone. After the war, while she was preaching, she heard the Holy Spirit say, "The German people are suffering from the deep scar of the way. Go and preach the gospel to them."

Hearing that, Corrie went to Germany to preach. After one particular sermon on forgiveness, a lot of people wept as they confessed their sins. Many waited to shake her hand as she stepped down from the platform. While she greeted them joyfully one by one, a man appeared in the line, his hand outstretched. As soon as she saw him, she felt as if her heart had stopped beating. He had been a guard at Ravensbruck, the concentration camp where she and her sister had been incarcerated. The prisoners had to pass naked before him when they were taken to the camp, and he frequently cut the food supply.

Painful memories of those terrible years unfolded before Corrie like a panorama. The man did not recognize her as a prisoner, but she knew she could never forget his face, even in a dream. He told her that, since serving as a guard at Ravensbruck, he had become a Christian. "I know that God has forgiven me for the cruel things I did there, but I would like to hear it from your lips as well. Will you forgive me?"

The image of her sister's dead body passed before her eyes; the bitter memory of her own suffering was revived. Though it was only a few seconds, it seemed as if she stood there for years. Finally she prayed, "Lord, I cannot forgive this man. Help me!"

She determined that she could, at least, lift her hand. And as she did, the resurrection life of Jesus flowed into Corrie's heart, and she forgave the former guard. All the feelings of bitterness disappeared and were replaced with joy through the power of the Lord. She later said that she felt as if she had become ten years younger. For years after that Corrie traveled all over the world preaching the love and forgiveness of Christ.

The forgiver always bears a responsibility: to throw self before the cross, crucifying self-centeredness, pride, wrath and self-assertions. When we do this, God abundantly pours in His resurrection life, His healing. Relationships come to life again—between parents and children, between friends—changing our lives into new ones. When our old wounds are healed and we are freed from any hatred, we can enjoy true happiness and joy.

Numerous people suffer needlessly with physical diseases caused by enmity and hatred. Family relationships are broken due to grudges and hate. How many parents are estranged from their children, how many friendships are cooled, because of hate and spite? Forgiveness is the only indispensable element of healing for us.

Praying in accordance with the teaching of our Lord Jesus—"Forgive us our debts, as we forgive our debtors"—is the key that will enable us to lead happy lives. Real freedom follows this kind of prayer and forgiveness.

The Lord taught us that we should forgive and be reconciled before we offer our sacrifices. Matthew 5:23,24 says, "Therefore if thou bring thy gift to the altar, and there rememberest that thy brother hath ought against thee; leave there thy gift before the altar, and go thy way; first be reconciled to thy brother, and then come and offer thy gift."

God answers the prayer of one who forgives and is reconciled. If we have grudges and hatred in our hearts, God cannot hear our prayers, however fervently we cry to Him. As the Lord said, we should see to it that the forgiveness of God overflows in us by forgiving those who committed sins against us.

"Forgive us our debts, as we forgive our debtors." When we pray this verse of the Lord's prayer day and night, our spirits, souls, bodies and daily living will be healed. Then with faith, hope and love flowing abundantly among us, we will always be able to march forward to a better tomorrow even if we still have sinful tendencies or shortcomings, even if we have personality clashes or differences of opinions.

5

Lead Us Not Into Temptation

God is our Father. We are the children of God almighty and omnipotent. As children plead earnestly for help and protection from danger, we can pray to God that He would lead us not into temptation.

But before we pray this prayer, we must have a correct understanding of the word *temptation* which Jesus used. Does God want to deliver us from temptation? Is He able to do so? What can we do to keep from falling into temptation?

The word *temptation* isn't heard too often in non-Christian circles. But Christians frequently say things like, "Deacon So-and-So has fallen into temptation." "I have overcome temptation." "Pray so that you may not fall into temptation."

Most of us use this word without fully understanding its deep meaning. What does *temptation* mean? There are two Greek words that are translated. One, *dokimadzo*, refers to the *test* to which God puts us to bring greater blessings to us by approving us and recognizing us.

If we endeavor to lead victorious lives, God will test us with *dokimadzo*. He wants to try us so He can reward us with good things, so He can recognize us and qualify us for greater blessings or usefulness to Him. To put an ox to a test so people can see that it is a good ox is the test of *dokimadzo*. The devil never puts us to this test which proves our qualification for a reward. This is not the meaning of *temptation* that we'll discuss here in terms of the Lord's prayer.

The other Greek word refers to the temptation attended by trial, suffering and tribulation. Sometimes this kind of temptation, *peiradzo*, is of God and sometimes it is of Satan. Let's look at the different motives involved.

The word that Jesus used in "lead us not into temptation" refers to the temptation that steals, kills and destroys the people who fall into it. Few people who have gone through this temptation remain in good condition.

God's will is that we will not fall into temptation that would destroy us through suffering, trial and tribulation. Christ's charge that we should pray that we may not fall into temptation shows the will of our loving God to hear our prayer. As we pray that we may not fall into temptation, we must have faith that through that prayer the outstretched hand of almighty God will deliver us from the temptation of the devil.

Trial, Suffering and Tribulation That God Allows

There are times when God makes us undergo trials, suffering and tribulation so He can determine our faithfulness. If we say, "Lord, Lord," with our lips but live lies, He allows us to undergo temptation in order that He may distinguish our truthfulness.

While the children of Israel wandered in the wilderness for forty years, God tried them. Though they said, "Lord," with their lips, their hearts were far from God. When things went well, they praised God, but when circumstances went badly, they turned their backs on Him. Because of this tendency, God tried the children of Israel to know whether or not they sincerely trusted in Him. Consequently, all the people except Joshua and Caleb who came out of Egypt died in the wilderness. Though they reached the place where they could see Canaan, the land flowing with milk and honey, they could not enter it.

God also tempted Abraham with a trial of his obedience. God told Abraham to take his only son, Isaac, to a mountain in the land of Moriah and offer him as a sacrifice, a burnt offering. Isaac was born in Abraham's old age and nothing could have been a more severe trial and tribulation than this request. A storm rose in Abraham's heart. Despair flooded in.

Why did God put Abraham to such a great test of *peiradzo* to undergo trial, suffering and tribulation? Because Abraham was inclined to love Isaac more than God. Seeing that Abraham was in danger of betraying and disobeying Him, God decided to try him. Abraham successfully passed the test which was to determine whether or not he was obedient. In obedience to the commandment of God, Abraham brought his only son to the mountain, bound him and placed him on a pile of firewood.

89

Can you imagine the pain and anguish Abraham must have felt as a father as he lifted up a knife to kill Isaac? Seeing the true obedience of Abraham, God delivered him from the trouble and said, "That in blessing I will bless thee, and in multiplying I will multiply thy seed as the stars of the heaven, and as the sand which is upon the seashore" (Gen. 22:17).

Of course it would have been much better for Abraham if he had not had to undergo such a trial. He was tried with *peiradzo* because he loved Isaac more than God, but he passed the trial successfully because of his faith, and therefore he received the blessing. God exempts us from this kind of test if we are wholeheartedly faithful to Him. And we are to pray that we will be faithful enough not to be led through this kind of test.

If we love the world more than God, He will even put us through trial, suffering and tribulation. Whenever we pray the prayer, "Lord, lead us not into temptation," we should examine our hearts with the question, "Lord, am I living an obedient life in the presence of God?"

The Temptation the Devil Gives

The devil tries to drive us into trial, tribulation and suffering also, but with a totally different intention. He wants to steal, kill and destroy us and our faith. Most of the *peiradzo* we undergo are from the devil. God seldom puts us to the test of trial, as He did Abraham.

When we endeavor to live in faith believing in Jesus as Savior, the devil tempts so he may remove this faith—by any and all means. The trial recorded in Hebrews 11:36-38 is this kind of test from the devil:

And others had trial of cruel mockings and scourgings. Yea, moreover of bonds and imprisonment.

They were stoned, they were sawn asunder, were tempted, were slain with the sword: they wandered about in sheepskins and goatskins; being destitute, afflicted, tormented; (of whom the world was not worthy:) they wandered in deserts, and in mountains, and in dens and caves of the earth.

These people had faith, but the devil shook them with trial, tribulation and suffering to take away their faith. Our Lord said that we should pray that we may not fall into this type of temptation prompted by Satan.

While Korea was under the Japanese rule for thirty-six years, the Japanese people imprisoned and killed many pastors and persecuted the leaders of the church. Satan caused Korea to undergo severe temptation—trial and tribulation—to stamp out Christianity. During the Korean War the communists came down and destroyed more than 260 churches. They shot and killed more than 230 pastors. They kidnapped many ministers and believers and took them to North Korea. This was also temptation or the trial of Satan. Our Lord said that we should pray that we would not fall into this temptation which would destroy the church and Christians, taking away the glory of God from this earth.

Concerning the temptation that the devil gives to the church, the Bible says, "Fear none of those things which thou shalt suffer: behold, the devil shall cast some of you into prison, that ye may be tried; and ye shall have tribulation ten days: be thou faithful unto death, and I will give thee a crown of life" (Rev. 2:10).

The devil tempts us to destroy us through weakening our faith, and he frantically tempts us to make us fall into the snare of sin. Adam and Eve stumbled in this very temptation because of the lust of the flesh, the lust of the eyes and the pride of life.

When Jesus had fasted for forty days, Satan tried to tempt Him. Perceiving that Jesus was hungry, Satan tempted Him by challenging Him to turn the stones into bread. Then he tempted Jesus by taking Him to the pinnacle of the temple and telling Him to throw Himself down on the street below. A third time Satan tempted Jesus saying that he would give Him all the kingdoms of the world if he would fall down and worship him.

Even today our enemy uses various means to trap us in his snare. If we are caught in such a temptation, we will be broken and trampled down in misery. This is why our Lord told us to pray that we might not fall into temptation.

Why Do We Fall Into *Peiradzo*?

According to James 1:14-15, "But every man is tempted, when he is drawn away of his own lust, and enticed. Then when lust hath conceived, it bringeth forth sin: and sin, when it is finished, bringeth forth death."

God allows us to undergo trial and affliction (even though we get hurt and suffer severe pain), for He wants us to see where we are in our relationship with Him. He wants us to repent and turn from the road leading to destruction before our lust conceives and brings forth sin and finally death.

The devil, however, tempts us when our faith becomes weak. The devil tempts when we fail to read the Scriptures, when we neglect praying, when we are no longer being filled with the Holy Spirit and when our service to God grows less enthusiastic. If our faith gradually cools down and our love toward God is replaced by our love toward the world, if we begin to walk in the counsel of the ungodly, stand in the way of sinners and sit in the seat of the scornful, we will fall into Satan's temptation.

If we are caught in this snare of temptation, we are robbed of our faith and doomed.

The devil tries to tempt us with appetite, greed for money and lust of the flesh. Since we received these desires from God, it is natural for us to enjoy them within the limit appointed by God. Our desire to wear good clothes or to live in comfortable homes is not bad in itself. And power obtained by legal means is God-given. But when we go beyond God's limits and become gluttons who live to eat or become overwhelmed by greed to make money by fair or foul means, the devil gets a toehold and leads us to the endless pit of destruction. What a great number of people fall to destruction due to their illicit fortune making, indulging in luxury and theft.

When we are driven by the appetite for power and consumed by pride, the devil's temptation wins. Attempts to take power by illegal means, as President Kim Il-Sung of North Korea did by sacrificing countless lives in order to satisfy his personal ambition, belong to the pride of this world. One who falls prey to this temptation becomes subject to the judgment of God and comes to ruin. Those who are driven by the lust of the flesh, the lust of the eyes and the pride of this world seem to live in comfort, glory and honor, but God who sees all things judges them; their pleasure is merely temporary.

How Can We Keep From Falling Into Temptation?

Jesus said that we should pray lest we should fall into the temptation of trial, tribulation and suffering, whether it is what God has permitted or what the devil has brought upon us. If we pray, God will hold us lest we should fall into the snare.

How then can God keep us from falling into the

temptation which leads to tribulation, suffering and ruin and which steals, kills and destroys us? We should bear in mind several things so that we can bear up successfully when temptation comes.

Knowledge of the Word of God
First, we must have a knowledge of the Word of God. When Jesus finished fasting forty days and Satan led Him into temptation, Jesus did not stand by any theories. He rejected the temptation of the devil by quoting, "It is written...." The Word of God is the wisdom of all wisdom and the knowledge of all knowledge. It did and does shine light in the darkness.

When Satan tried to ensnare Jesus by asking Him to turn a stone into bread, Jesus answered, "It is written, Man shall not live by bread alone, but by every word that proceedeth out of the mouth of God" (Matt. 4:4).

When Satan tried to ensnare Jesus on the pinnacle of the temple, Jesus again quoted the Word. Satan challenged,

> If thou be the Son of God, cast thyself down: for it is written, He shall give his angels charge concerning thee: and in their hands they shall bear thee up, lest at any time thou dash thy foot against a stone. Jesus said unto him, It is written again, Thou shalt not tempt the Lord thy God (Matt. 4:6,7).

Satan then took Jesus up to a high mountain and showed him all the kingdoms of the world. He said he would give them all to Jesus if He would only fall down and worship Satan. This time Jesus answered, "It is written, Thou shall worship the Lord thy God, and him only shalt thou serve" (Matt. 4:10).

Satan then left Jesus, and angels came and ministered

unto Him. If we treasure every scripture, from Genesis to Revelation, we can always defeat Satan's most deceptive snares because we will be able to see the trap.

One day a man came to me for counsel. He said, "Pastor, I have two wives. After my legal marriage, I set up another home with another woman with whom I worked. Both women love me and I love both of them. I cannot give up either of them and each says she cannot live without me. Since I work hard to support both homes and go back and forth between them, I think I am charitable and doing the right thing, yet I think about it and lie awake at night."

He was obviously caught in the snare of the devil but not aware of it. I countered, "Have you ever listened to the Word of God? One of the Ten Commandments says that we should not commit adultery; and Jesus also said that we should not commit adultery, which is what you are doing."

"What shall I do then? If I stop going to either of the households, that woman will starve to death. And there are children."

"Adjust your life in such a way as not to violate the law and morality. You could provide a living for the woman and schooling for the children whose relationship you have to sever. When you do so, you can be right before God."

If we have a sure knowledge of the Word of God, we can resist the devil resolutely no matter how subtly he may try to ensnare us. When we do not rely upon the Word, but try to solve our problems in our own way and with our own human wisdom, we fall into the devil's snare.

Live by Faith
Second, we should live by faith. When the devil tempts

95

us, he causes uneasiness and fear. Based on our surroundings—what we see, hear and touch—Satan whispers, "You have failed. Now you shall die. You are
ruined. Everything is finished."

If we live by faith, however, we can boldly confess
our faith and march forward saying, "I believe," even
when there is no encouraging sign to see, hear or touch.
Why? Because our faith is founded on the Word of God
which will not pass away. When we move forward
holding the word of promise, we can pass through the
dark tunnel into the bright outside. The words of man
and the kingdom of this earth will pass away; the trend
of the times will change. But not a jot or tittle of the
Word of God will be abolished. To stand firm against
temptation, we should live by faith, the foundation of
which is the Word of God.

Be Faithful to God

We must be faithful to God. Everybody is committed
and dedicated to something. One lives for money;
another for power. Some live for pleasure and others are
consumed by an urge to gamble. Whatever it may be,
everyone has one thing for which he or she lives. We
Christians, however, should first be faithful to the altar
of God; we should seek the kingdom of God and His
righteousness. We should love God and follow Him with
all our hearts, souls and minds. When we do so, God
helps us not to fall into temptation. If God is not at the
center of our lives, we will fall into the temptation
allowed by God and that instigated by the devil.

Persevere and Give Thanks

When trial does come to you, do not complain and
murmur. When we do this, we are soon talking more
about the devil than about Jesus.

When the children of Israel were tried in the wilderness, they continually murmured, complained and sighed. They did not acknowledge that God was still leading them. Consequently they were utterly destroyed. Even if your murmuring and complaining can be justified, discipline your thoughts because murmuring and fault finding provide the devil with good opportunity to destroy you. As you learn to give thanks for everything, you receive God's help to overcome temptation.

An American man was sentenced to fifty years in prison when he was forty years old. There seemed to be no possibility of his being released, and at first he raged and fumed. He kicked the cell door and shook the bars of the window. He spat, raved and yelled like a mad man. But after a few days of such rage he realized that it was useless. At that moment he found a Bible in a corner of the cell and began to read it. In those pages he found Jesus to whom he confessed all his sins, spending several days in tears.

His outlook changed. He no longer felt a stifling hopelessness, nor did he feel cramped in the prison cell. Though he was in prison, he felt freer than he could imagine possible. He also experienced a joy that he had never before felt. He began to leap and roll on the cell floor out of joy and thanksgiving.

Eventually he learned that his wife and daughter were ill with cancer. Though he had the responsibility to take care of them as husband and father, he was helpless in the prison. He felt deep frustration, but it was useless to complain. Rather, he said, "Since there is nothing I can do, why shouldn't I give thanks even for this illness?" So he gave thanks saying, "Lord, I thank You that my wife has cancer. I also thank You that my daughter has cancer." But a wonderful thing happened. After a while he received word that his wife and daughter had been completely healed, and because he was a model prisoner, his prison term was reduced to ten years, then to five years.

Thanksgiving is a shortcut to overcoming temptation. The advice I give to those who come to me for counseling is: Give thanks in all things. Whether a husband and wife have quarreled or their child has run away from home, whether one has been stricken with a fatal disease or had a business failure, Romans 8:28 should be received with faith: "All things work together for good to them that love God, to them who are the called according to his purpose."

Health is not the only thing that works together for good; illness works together for good. Not only business success, but also failure works together for good. Not only the praise of others, but also their complaints work together for good.

When Joseph was sold into slavery by his elder brothers, he was seventeen years old. He was a slave for fifteen years, spending two of them in prison on a false charge. It seemed that his life had been ruined. But Joseph did not murmur or complain. Rather he continued to give thanks to God.

Eventually Joseph was chosen to be the highest in command under the Egyptian pharaoh. Because of a famine, Joseph's older brothers came to Egypt to buy food. How surprised they were to meet Joseph. They fell down before him, as they were so grateful for his generosity. Through his help, they moved to Egypt, but when their father, Jacob, died, the brothers feared Joseph might take revenge on them. But Joseph saw things differently. He said, "But as for you, ye thought evil against me: but God meant it unto good, to bring to pass, as it is this day, to save much people alive" (Gen. 50:20).

However hard others may try to bring evil against you,

God turns that evil into good, if you are a Christian and trust Him to work out everything for good. Those foolish people who accept only sweet-tasting morsels and spit out all the bitter herbs cannot help but fall into temptation. God works everything together for our good.

We have to look at the total picture of our past, present and future. Thank God that you have quarreled with your wife. If your children have left your home kicking the door hard, offer a prayer of thanksgiving: "Father, my son has left home. Though I don't know where he is, I thank You. If You make him come back home again, I will give You more thanks." If your business does not run smoothly, give thanks. The Bible says, "He who sacrifices thank offerings honors me, and he prepares the way so that I may show him the salvation of God" (Ps. 50:23, NIV). This scripture tells us that the sacrifice of thanksgiving prepares the way for God to send His divine help quickly. Therefore we should give thanks in everything so we do not fall into temptation.

Remember, God, our good Father, does not want us to come to destruction through suffering, trial and tribulation. Jesus commanded that we always ask God to keep us from this temptation.

If we disobey God and become full of greed, God allows us this temptation of *peiradzo*. But most of the trials that come to us are brought on us by the devil who tries to steal, kill and destroy us. When we indulge in lust because of our weak faith, the devil jumps at us with a snare which can destroy us.

As Jesus taught us we should pray, "Lead us not into temptation." With the sure knowledge of the Word of God in our hearts, we should keep our faith firm, avoiding temptation by giving constant thanks to God for all things. But even if we happen to encounter temptation, we needn't be trapped by it, as we have a God who can deliver us from evil.

6

But Deliver Us From Evil

No one can deny the fact that good and evil exist. But when Adam and Eve lived in the Garden of Eden, they knew only everlasting love, obedience and spiritual fellowship. Only when Adam and Eve fell, did evil and its force flood this world.

In spite of severe laws and penalties, evil is multiplying like an epidemic. But what is in the center of evil?

The sixth point Jesus taught in His prayer is "deliver us from evil." The original Greek for this passage means "deliver us from the hand of the wicked," and *the wicked* refers to the devil or Satan. Let's examine the origin of the wicked one, his activities and our resistance to him.

The Origin of the Wicked

People ask repeatedly, "Why has God made the wicked enemy, the devil, and allowed him to wreak havoc in the world?" But God did not make the evil one.

The Bible says that the first state of the devil was not evil. He was created by God as an archangel from the cherubim. He had the highest position in heaven; he was responsible for guarding the holiness of God. But when pride prompted him to try to usurp the authority of God, he fell and changed into the wicked Satan. The Bible says this about Lucifer before he fell and became Satan:

> Thou hast been in Eden the garden of God; every precious stone was thy covering, the sardius, topaz, and the diamond, and the beryl, the onyx, and the jasper, the sapphire, the emerald, and the carbuncle, and gold: the workmanship of thy tabrets and of thy pipes was prepared in thee in the day that thou wast created. Thou art the anointed cherub that covereth; and I have set thee so: thou wast upon the holy mountain of God; thou hast walked up and down in the midst of the stones of fires (Ezek. 28:13,14).

This scripture shows that in the beginning, when God created the heaven and earth, the planet was occupied by Satan. The earth we now inhabit is not the original earth created by God in Genesis 1:1.

Earth existed millions of years before man appeared. And the archangel who took charge of this earth was Lucifer.

Before he fell, Lucifer ruled this earth according to the will of God. Lucifer praised God with beautiful songs and gave glory to God. But as soon as pride arose from his heart causing him to rebel against God, God drove him out of the old Eden and passed dire judgment on him. The old earth became without form and void; and darkness was upon the face of the deep. Lucifer became Satan and took the power of the air.

The assertion of anthropologists that the origin of animal life on earth goes back billions of years (based on the datings of excavated fossils or bones) does not conflict with the record of the Bible. In that earth, that first Eden where Lucifer ruled, there were mountains and streams, plants and trees. Some theologians maintain that there were also human beings. But because of the fall of Lucifer, God pronounced a fearful judgment on earth which caused disorder. All the mountains, streams, plants and trees were buried, and fossils and petroleum are the remains of animals that lived in this first Eden.

Genesis 1:2 describes the scene in which the earth underwent transformation: "And the earth was without form, and void; and darkness was upon the face of the deep. And the Spirit of God moved upon the water." After God transformed the earth which had been in the midst of chaos God created Adam and Eve and put them there to live.

The earth God transformed into the second Eden is now about 6,000 years old. And tempting Adam and Eve, Lucifer, in the form of a serpent, again changed this transformed earth into the miserable world we know today.

Why did Lucifer become the devil? Ezekiel 28 goes on to describe the situation further:

Thou Lucifer wast perfect in thy ways from the day that thou wast created, till iniquity was found in thee. By the multitude of thy merchandise they have filled the midst of thee with violence, and thou hast sinned: therefore I will cast thee as profane out of the mountain of God: and I will destroy thee, O covering cherub, from the midst of the stones of fire. Thine heart was lifted up because of thy beauty, thou hast corrupted thy wisdom by reason of thy brightness: I will cast thee to the ground, I will lay thee before kings, that they may behold thee (vv. 15-17).

The fall of Lucifer and his banishment from the old Eden, the former earth, was caused by pride. As Proverbs says, "Pride goeth before destruction, and an haughty spirit before a fall" (16:18). Isaiah wrote concerning the pride of Lucifer:

How art thou fallen from heaven, O Lucifer, son of the morning! How art thou cut down to the ground, which didst weaken the nations! For thou hast said in thine heart, I will ascend into heaven, I will exalt my throne above the stars of God: I will sit also upon the mount of the congregation, in the sides of the north: I will ascend above the heights of the clouds; I will be like the most High. Yet thou shalt be brought down to hell, to the sides of the pit (14:12-15).

How can the creature, the son of the morning, sit upon the same position as the Creator? How can the creature behave like the Creator? The apostle Paul warns lest we be "lifted up with pride" and "fall into the condemnation of the devil" (1 Tim. 3:6). This means that the sin by which the devil was condemned was just this: pride.

Where have the numerous evil spirits and demons come from? The Bible answers this question: "And there appeared another wonder in heaven; and behold a great red dragon, having seven heads and ten horns, and seven crowns upon his heads. And his tail drew the third part

of the stars of heaven, and did cast them to the earth"
(Rev. 12:3,4).

The dragon in heaven signifies Satan, who fell taking
one-third of the heavenly host with him. These fallen
angels are in the world, interfering with the work of God,
causing trouble to God's people and striving to lead
unbelievers to the path of destruction.

The Works of Satan and His Followers

Satan and his followers do evil not only on the individual level, but also on the state and international
level; they can and do incite an individual or a nation
to rebel against God; they allure a people with atheism;
they lead a people to moral depravity and economic
destruction. Jesus said, "The thief cometh not, but for
to steal, and to kill, and to destroy" (John 10:10). Let
us examine the work of Satan and his followers in the
Bible.

Unclean Spirits

The Bible says, "And when he [Jesus] had called unto
him his twelve disciples, he gave them power against
unclean spirits, to cast them out, and to heal all manner
of sickness and all manner of disease" (Matt. 10:1).

Look at the torrent of filth, lewdness and moral
depravity that sweeps the world.

I was alarmed to hear the following story recently. It
is said that in Korea's high-class gisaeng houses and bars
people are giving themselves unrestrained to sumptuous
feasts of liquor and sex; even in the daytime, filthy, ob-
scene and lewd behavior is committed. Now unless such
lewdness, wantonness and corrupt practices of the rich
and powerful are stopped, they will rapidly become ram-
pant like an epidemic and will devastate our whole land.

From where does such moral depravity and lasciviousness come? From unclean spirits working behind the scenes. These evil spirits degrade households and the society as well as individuals.

Unless we Christians renovate the atmosphere of our own household and purify the atmosphere of our society by casting out all unclean spirits, we cannot keep the minds of our children from being defiled by the wickedness flooding our cities like a river overflowing its banks. The church must arise and bind these unclean spirits with faith and prayer, for this cannot be done by mere human strength and ability.

Evil Spirits

An evil spirit makes us rebel. It troubles our hearts, making us victims of envy and jealousy; it causes destructive divisions in our minds. King Saul had such an evil spirit: "But the Spirit of the Lord departed from Saul, and an evil spirit from the Lord troubled him" (1 Sam. 16:14).

If Hitler had not been possessed by an evil spirit, he would never have started the war or massacred millions of people. In Germany, I once heard that the carpet on the floor of Hitler's airplane was torn to pieces as if it had been cut by a sharp knife; I was told that Hitler had torn the carpet to pieces with his fingernails. It is said that even the dinner table was marred by the splashes of his tears. As the result of being possessed by an evil spirit, Hitler devastated Europe and massacred six million Jews.

The mass suicide of the group called the People's Temple is another incident where an occultist was possessed by an evil spirit. Jim Jones, their leader, convinced some 900 people to drink cyanide-laced Kool-aid. What a dreadful and harmful ending heresy and strange doctrines can have.

National governmental authorities should examine closely the heresy and strange doctrines of such groups and root them out for the sake of sanity of the people. Who can guarantee us that such an incident will not happen again?

The New Testament also refers to the evil spirits that bring madness to people. "When the even was come, they brought unto him many that were possessed with devils: and he cast out the spirits with his word, and healed all that were sick" (Matt. 8:16).

There has been no time in history when evil spirits have prevailed as much as they do now. Mental hospitals around the world are full. My mail from many countries confirms an overriding problem: With the surge of urbanization and industrialization, men and women are feeling like components of a machine. They are suffering from spiritual barrenness, groaning under the heavy burden of mind. Capitalizing on this moment, evil spirits come in quickly, bringing uneasiness, fretfulness, disappointment and frustration to non-believers. And they even cause split-personalities. How grateful we Christians should be; we can resist the enemy when we feel oppression trying to overtake us.

Lying and Seducing Spirits

A lying spirit entices people to believe in a lie, and then the lying spirit leads them to destruction. "And he said, I will go out, and be a lying spirit in the mouth of all his prophets. And the Lord said, Thou shalt entice him, and thou shalt also prevail: go out, and do even so" (2 Chron. 18:21).

Jesus our Lord is the way, the truth and the life. Those who have Jesus at the center of their hearts will inherit everlasting life. But those who are deceived by lying spirits, those who live only for the sake of the lust of their flesh, lust of their eyes and pleasures of the world, will fall into eternal destruction.

Similar to lying spirits are seducing spirits. "Now the Spirit speaketh expressly, that in the latter times some shall depart from the faith, giving heed to seducing spirits, and doctrines of devils" (1 Tim. 4:1).

Today, these seducing spirits and doctrines of devils prevail. Communism is the worst kind of a seducing spirit and demonic teaching in human history. Communists publicize a paradise where everyone enjoys equality and freedom. But when one looks on the inside of these countries, one finds that most of the people live in a miserable state of slavery without having any freedom of the press or freedom to move about—while only a few in the ruling class satisfy their desires.

These seducing spirits and doctrines of devils are also in religious circles. Someone may say that people cannot have everlasting life unless they assemble to a certain place—where the millennial kingdom will come. Of course this is a lie, but a seducing spirit can convince people that lies are full of truth.

The Spirit of Divination

"And it came to pass, as we went to prayer, a certain damsel possessed with a spirit of divination met us, which brought her masters much gain by soothsaying" (Acts 16:16).

At the beginning of every new year, many nonbelievers—politicians, businessmen, the rich and the poor—are busy consulting fortune tellers. They go to diviners expecting to hear that they will have good luck despite their uneasiness about the future. But then, after they've heard of good fortune, they restlessly wonder

108

if the information they received is true. Christians should be careful not to fall into such delusion. Blessings follow us naturally when we live diligently in faith, hope and love—believing in God and following Jesus. God's Word declares it is so.

Spirits That Cause Physical Maladies

The devil also causes blindness and dumbness. "Then was brought unto him one possessed with a devil, blind, and dumb: and he healed him, insomuch that the blind and dumb spake and saw" (Matt. 12:22).

Of course not all blind and dumb people are possessed by the devil. Some are born without optic nerves or have underdeveloped vocal organs. But many people become blind or dumb when they are possessed by the devil.

I have seen a dumb person whose case was so grave that doctors had given up hope of any cure. But when I prayed for him in the name of Jesus, his tongue was loosed and he spoke again. I have also seen a blind person, who had no hope of ever seeing, open his eyes with sight when an evil spirit was cast out in the name of Jesus.

Concerning the deaf spirit the Bible says, "When Jesus saw that the people came running together, he rebuked the foul spirit, saying unto him, Thou dumb and deaf spirit, I charge thee, come out of him, and enter no more into him" (Mark 9:25).

Of course there are those who were born without eardrums and whose eardrums have been ruptured. But there are those who cannot hear because of deaf spirits. And if these spirits are cast out in the name of Jesus, hearing can be restored miraculously and immediately.

The Bible says that the devil causes all manner of diseases. "How God anointed Jesus of Nazareth with the Holy Ghost and with power: who went about doing good, and healing all that were oppressed of the devil;

for God was with him" (Acts 10:38).

Diseases caused by the devil can be cured temporarily by an operation or by the use of drugs. But more fundamental treatment is to drive out the devil in earnest prayer, for then health is restored naturally.

The Personality of the Devil

Followers of liberal theology try not to recognize the presence of the devil as one who has personality. They ascribe the existence of evil to the social structure, to bad politics and to unequal distribution of wealth. This thought is far from the teachings of the Bible. If the contention of these people is true, why does the suicide rate increase yearly and lewdness and dissipation prevail in Scandinavian countries that have good social structures and environments? What about the communist countries that claim they have equal distribution or the United States that boasts of material affluence?

Evil prevails on this earth, not because of bad social systems nor because of unfair distribution. But because the devil, the source of all evil, exists. Wherever the devil is, evil always follows in many disguises.

In the Old Testament, Adam fell by the intrigue of the devil. At his hand, Job fell to the pit of misery, and David was also sorely tempted. In the New Testament, the devil tempted Jesus; he entered into the heart of Judas Iscariot, making him betray Jesus. The apostles, Peter, Paul and James, warned us repeatedly against the work of the devil. "Be sober, be vigilant; because your adversary the devil, as a roaring lion, walketh about, seeking whom he may devour: whom resist steadfast in the faith, knowing that the same afflictions are accomplished in your brethren that are in the world" (1 Pet. 5:8,9). "For we wrestle not against flesh and blood, but against principalities, against powers, against the rulers of the darkness of this world, against spiritual wickedness in high places" (Eph. 6:12). "Submit yourselves therefore to God. Resist the devil, and he will flee from you" (James 4:7).

So far we have seen the work of the devil and his followers. But this knowledge is not all we need. We need to resist the attacks of the devil and his followers who incessantly seek our lives. We must drive out the devil if he is causing trouble in our environment and families.

We Are the Winners

In these last days evil spirits, knowing their time is short, are making a desperate endeavor to cause trouble to Christians who are earnestly seeking God. The way to drive out the devil and his evil spirits is no other than through fasting and prayer.

When evil spirits derange our lives or when a big and urgent problem approaches us, we must fast and pray, suppressing all our desires as we entreat God. Fasting helps us to concentrate our thoughts upon God and opens the channel for us to receive maximum power from God. When the disciples asked why they had not been able to cast out an evil spirit, Jesus answered, "Howbeit this kind goeth not out but by prayer and fasting" (Matt. 17:21).

But we must never forget that Satan is defeated. Making a public spectacle of evil principalities and powers trying to steal, kill and destroy us, Jesus disarmed and triumphed over them on the cross.

"Blotting out the handwriting of ordinances that was against us, which was contrary to us, and took it out of the way, nailing it to his cross: and having spoiled principalities, and powers, he made a shew of them openly, triumphing over them in it" (Col. 2:14,15).

Satan is now powerless before Jesus and His name, because by His resurrection Jesus subdued death, the chief weapon of Satan. Satan and his followers no longer have any power over us who believe in Jesus Christ as Savior. We are given the authority of the name of Jesus, which can easily win over the power of Satan. Luke 10:18,19 says, "And he [Jesus] said unto them, I beheld Satan as lightning fall from heaven. Behold, I give unto you power [authority] to tread on serpents and scorpions, and over all the power of the enemy: and nothing shall by any means hurt you."

How great is that power! Those who accept Jesus as Savior and live close to Him have the "power to tread on serpents and scorpions, and over all the power of the enemy." The moment we believe in Jesus, we become winners. The Bible also says, "Ye are of God, little children, and have overcome them: because greater is he that is in you, than he that is in the world" (1 John 4:4).

God, who is omniscient, omnipotent and omnipresent and before whom nothing of this world can stand, is in our hearts—in person. Therefore, though the devil and his evil spirits come from one direction, they will flee away in seven directions.

Jesus taught us who have become the children of God to pray that we might be delivered from evil. This is the privilege entitled to the children of God. If the children of God are still oppressed by the devil, it is a shameful thing that grieves God.

Every day we should not fail to pray that God deliver us from evil for then our families, our children, our societies and our nations will triumph—being delivered from the hand of the wicked. Since we know the true character of the devil, our enemy, let us arm ourselves incessantly with the Word and with prayer. The Holy Spirit has promised to help us. Our spirits, souls and environment can become well—day by day in the blessings of God.

7

Jesus Who Will Come Again

So far we have set our thoughts on the Word so we can pray as Jesus taught us. Having Jesus within us, we can pray that the name of the Father and the will of His kingdom might be glorified and come among us. We can pray to our good God to give us our daily bread to forgive our sins and to deliver us from evil. But does our prayer to God the Father end here? No. At the close of His prayer Jesus taught us how to think in relation to the future world. Let's look at these points.

The Kingdom, Power and Glory

"For thine is the kingdom, and the power, and the glory, for ever."

The meaning of this verse, Matthew 6:13, is that the kingdom, the power and the glory of this world, past, present and future, belong to God. The supreme ruler of all things is God the Father. King David, the bravest and the greatest among the kings of Judah, praised God along these lines when he handed his throne down to his son Solomon, entrusting him with the task of building the temple of God:

> Thine, O Lord, is the greatness, and the power, and the glory, and the victory, and the majesty: for all that is in the heaven and in the earth is thine; thine is the kingdom, O Lord, and thou art exalted as head above all. Both riches and honor come of thee, and thou reignest over all; and in thine hand is power and might; and in thine hand it is to make great, and to give strength unto all (1 Chron. 29:11).

God is holding all the authority in His hand today and will take it to Himself at the last day to build His kingdom, namely the new heaven and the new earth. Consequently, when we pray, "For thine is the kingdom, and the power, and the glory, for ever," we must picture the new heaven and the new earth which will be made by the sovereign power of God. It is especially important that we who live now, when the coming of the Lord is close at hand, should accurately know what will come to pass in the last days so that we can pray in line with God's will.

When Jesus was looking at the Jerusalem temple, His disciples asked Him, "And what shall be the sign of thy coming, and of the end of the world?" (Matt. 24:3).

Jesus answered, "Take heed that no man deceive you. For many shall come in my name saying I am Christ; and shall deceive many. And ye shall hear of wars and rumors

116

of wars" (Matt. 24:4-6). He went on to say that there will be worldwide unrest, and that persecution will come upon those who believe in Him. There will be famines and earthquakes. The gospel shall be preached in all the world for a witness unto all nations. Then shall the end come.

Two thousand years have passed since the disciples asked Jesus this question on the Mount of Olives. Both history and our experience indicate that all these prophesied signs of the last days are unfolding. More false prophets have risen than at any other time in history. They have persecuted the church, the body of Christ, and seduced it. Wars, persecutions and earthquakes have broken out and the gospel of Jesus Christ is being preached to all the nations of the world. The end, which our Lord referred to in His prophecy, is 2,000 years closer than when the disciples lived. And now we can still ask the same question of Jesus: "Lord, what shall be the sign of thy coming, and of the end of the world?"

God's Word still explains what will come to pass in the last days and His plan for the end of the world.

Old Testament Prophecy Concerning the Last Days

The Old Testament book of Daniel, which was written 2,000 years ago, accurately records the events of our present age—as if an historian had written of past events. Through the image King Nebuchadnezzar saw in Daniel 2:36-45 the Holy Spirit reveals to us the whole history of Europe—till the end of the world.

About 600 years before Christ, King Nebuchadnezzar, who ruled the immense Babylonian Empire, had a fearful and terrible nightmare, but when he awoke in the morning, he couldn't remember any of the dream. The king gathered all his magicians, astrologers and sorcerers and commanded them—under threat of death—to recall the dream and give him its interpretation. Daniel and three young men, Shadrach, Meshach and Abednego, Jews who had been taken captive from Israel, also were under this threat when God the Father, who heard the prayers of Daniel and his friends, showed Daniel King Nebuchadnezzar's dream and gave Daniel the wisdom to interpret it. That dream was a synopsis of world history from the time of Babylon to the end of the world. Daniel went forward in the presence of the king and said:

> Thou, O king, sawest, and behold a great image... This image's head was of fine gold, his breast and his arms of silver, his belly and his thighs of brass, his legs of iron, his feet part of iron and part of clay. Thou sawest till that a stone was cut out without hands, which smote the image upon his feet...and broke them to pieces. Then was the iron, the clay, the brass, the silver, and the gold broken to pieces, and became like the chaff of the summer threshing floors...and the stone that smote the image became a great mountain, and filled the whole earth (Dan. 2:31-35).

Yes, the king knew this is what he had dreamed, and he then accepted the interpretation Daniel gave: Nebuchadnezzar was the gold head of this image. And, Daniel told him, "After thee shall arise another kingdom inferior to thee," made of silver and divided in two. But this kingdom was to perish and a kingdom of brass, stronger than silver, was to take its place, which in turn was to fall to a kingdom of iron, stronger than the kingdom of brass and divided into two. Finally, the earth was to be ruled by a kingdom of "ten toes."

Daniel's interpretation has been proven through

history. As Daniel said, Babylon soon fell to the Medes and Persians and these two kingdoms ruled Babylon alternately. The Medes and Persians were the two silver arms of the statue. Beneath the breast of silver was the belly of brass, the Hellenistic period of Alexander the Great of Macedonia who conquered the Medes and Persians. This kingdom of brass reached not only to the belly, but to the thighs, which indicated Rome which rose at the third century before Christ. Rome conquered Greece and took control over the whole Western world, but it was soon divided in two, the Eastern empire and the Western empire. The Western Roman Empire fell in 476 A.D., and the Eastern empire fell in 1453 A.D.

Now only one period remains—the period of the ten toes when the ten nations of Europe are reunited around the region that was once Babylon. From that moment, the end of the world begins. Daniel's interpretation refers to a stone—Jesus Christ who shall come again at the end of the world. Isaiah also refers to this stone: "Behold, I lay in Zion for a foundation a stone, a tried stone, a precious corner stone, a sure foundation: he that believeth shall not make haste" (Is. 28:16).

When Jesus Christ returns to this earth, smiting and judging the "toes" of the feet, human history shall come to an end. Just as the stone filled the whole earth, so the kingdom of Jesus Christ, the everlasting kingdom of God, shall cover the earth.

God revealed this synopsis of human history a second time in order to reinforce the validity of this revelation.

The second revelation is recorded in Daniel 7:1-14. This was the first year of the reign of King Belshazzar, the grandson of King Nebuchadnezzar. This time God spoke about the future things in animal imagery.

In a dream Daniel saw four great beasts come out from the sea. The first was a lion with the wings of an eagle, representing Nebuchadnezzar. The eagle wings meant that he conquered and ruled the whole world quickly.

The second beast was like a bear raised up on one side and eating three ribs. The body raised up to one side means that, though it was the united kingdom of the Medes and Persians, Persia took ascendancy over the Medes. The three ribs in the mouth signified the three peaceful kingdoms to be occupied by the Medes and Persians—Babylon, Lybia and Egypt.

The third beast was a leopard with four wings and four heads. No one would compete with such a fast animal: Alexander the Great and the four generals under him. At the age of thirty he conquered the Medes and Persians. He marched to what we know as Syria, Egypt and Iran, putting them all under the hoofs of his horse. When he died of fever, however, the kingdom was divided into four parts by his generals. And the four kingdoms fought fiercely, biting and tearing each other until they were finally conquered by Rome.

The fourth beast Daniel saw was dreadful and terrible with iron teeth; it devoured and trampled down everything it could reach. This was the image of Rome conquering the immense territory from Europe to the border of India—the largest empire in human history.

When Daniel was gazing at this beast's horns, a little horn came up among the ten and plucked out three by the roots. In this little horn were eyes like those of a man, and a mouth speaking great things. And when they appeared the judgment began.

Daniel's vision also shows that ten nations will be united on the former Roman territory. The toes of the statue's feet in Nebuchadnezzar's dream and the ten horns of this beast indicate that ten European countries shall eventually be united. The little horn that came up among the ten horns symbolizes the anti-Christ who will come up among the ten countries and unite three of them into one. He will put the remaining seven in his hand and dictate to the whole world, speaking words that resist the Lord God until God finally judges him. In his vision Daniel clearly saw the image of God, the judge:

> I beheld till the thrones were cast down, and the Ancient of days did sit, whose garment was white as snow, and the hair of his head like the pure wool: his throne was like the fiery flame, and his wheels as burning fire. A fiery stream issued and came forth from before him: thousand thousands ministered unto him, and ten thousand times ten thousand stood before him: the judgment was set, and the books were opened. I beheld them because of the voice of the great words which the horn spake: I beheld even till the beast was slain, and his body destroyed, and given to the burning flame. As concerning the rest of the beasts, they had their dominion taken away: yet their lives were prolonged for a season and time. I saw in the night visions, and, behold, one like the Son of man came with the clouds of heaven, and came to the Ancient of days, and they brought him near before him. And there was given him dominion, and glory, and a kingdom, that all people, nations, and languages, should serve him: his dominion is an everlasting dominion, which shall not pass away, and his kingdom that which shall not be destroyed (Dan. 7:9-14).

This shows the millennial kingdom of Jesus Christ. God will take the antichrist and throw him into the lake of fire and brimstone. Those who follow the antichrist will also be thrown into the lake of fire, and Jesus will come to this earth and reign forever with the saints. In the past, people have not known when these things might happen. They read this with only vague understanding. But we who are living now witness the signs of our generation and are sure that the day of the Lord's coming is near.

Fulfillment of the Prophecy

Are we really in the end times? Is the former territory of the Roman Empire being restored? Will the age of ten toes or ten horns soon come into being? Is the appearance of the antichrist and the end of the world close at hand?

The Bible said that the most conspicuous sign of the end of the world would be the independence of Israel. In the year of 70 A.D., Israel was overrun and devastated by Rome as the recompense for crucifying Jesus. The Jews were scattered all over the world and lived as strangers and vagabonds for 2,000 years. Historically, the Israelites were a wandering homeless people, but on May 14, 1948, they established an independent national state headed by David Ben-Gurion.

Jesus said, "Now learn a parable of the fig tree; when his branch is yet tender, and putteth forth leaves, ye know that summer is nigh: so likewise ye, when ye shall see all these things, know that it is near, even at the doors" (Matt. 24:32-33). The budding fig tree symbolizes the restoration of Israel. Jesus Himself said that everyone should know that the Son of God is at the door when Israel becomes a nation again.

Thirty-nine years have now passed since the independence of Israel. In that time, the Arab states have made several unsuccessful attempts to destroy Israel. But Egypt, the leading Arab state, has concluded a goodwill treaty with Israel, fortifying her validity.

If God opens the door, no one can close it, and if He

closes a door, no one can open it. There will never be a nation that can destroy Israel—a people who gained their independence by the power of God. Israel will never perish because God prophesied that He would finally purify her by having her sign a seven-year treaty with the antichrist. Today, everyone who fights with Israel falls. The Soviets, allied with the hard-line Arab countries, are now trying to destroy Israel, but as a result of their efforts, the Soviets will disappear from this earth.

After God provided a homeland for Israel, He began to gather ten horns. Since World War II, Europe has always felt pressure from the Soviet Union on the north and by the United States on the west. Cornered economically, militarily and politically, Europe formed a unified organization; the former territory of the Roman Empire is once again being brought together.

Europe achieved economic unification by forming the European Economic Community in Brussels, Belgium, in 1958; Europe has promoted military unification by establishing the North Atlantic Treaty Organization (NATO); and the process is now underway to work out political unification. At present, twelve countries are united and the territory of the Roman Empire will soon re-emerge.

Daniel prophesied events 2,600 years ago that now are newspaper headlines.

The *Choong Ang Daily Newspaper* of Seoul, Korea, carried an article on December 23, 1986, entitled, "The Birth of the United States of Europe Is Impending."

It said that nearly all of the parliaments of the twelve EC countries had ratified the Treaty of Hague, officially titled the Treaty of Unified Europe.

The news article said the treaty calls for the following action of EC countries by 1992: "The people of the member states and their merchandise will freely come and go without any barrier or restriction; the people of the member nations will use the same passport under the name of the EC; the restriction of borders will be abolished in employment, and the labor market will be liberalized; the sole EC president will be elected by the European Parliament in the future; ECU (the European Currency Unit) which is now used as the means of money order will take the role of everyday currency within the EC.''

The EC has determined that in 1987 they will deregulate foreign exchange between countries, which should strengthen Europe as one large economic power rather than many small nations.

It is clear that Jesus is now knocking at the last door of history. Our saying that the Lord's coming is near at hand is not the dreamy remark of a mystic. The prophecy of the Bible is coming true before our eyes. The age in which we live is the period of the ten toes or horns.

How close are we to the end? The Bible says that the end of the world will come between the seven years from the moment unified Europe makes a seven-year treaty with independent Israel. Noteworthy progress has been made in combining Europe into one union, and when the Union of Europe is born, the head of the European Union will make a seven-year treaty with Israel. This fact is recorded in Daniel 9:27: "And he shall confirm the covenant with many for one week: and in the midst of the week he shall cause the sacrifice and the oblation to cease, and for the overspreading of abominations he shall make it desolate, even until the consummation, and that determined shall be poured upon the desolate."

This prophecy means that the leader of the European Union will make a seven-year treaty with Israel and then help Israel demolish the Arab temple (which now stands on Mount Zion) and build the temple of the Lord. During the first three-and-a-half years of the treaty, the antichrist will become close to Israel as if they were on a honeymoon. The Israelis will accept the antichrist as their Messiah who will make it possible for them to build the temple.

But a war will break out in the air after the first three-and-a-half years. It will be between Michael, the archangel of God, and the dragon, Satan. The dragon, not finding a place to abide in the air, will be cast down to this earth with his followers. The dragon will enter into the body of the antichrist and his image will be completely changed; he will start a campaign to extirpate Israel; he will set up an idol in the temple in Jerusalem and will have the Israelites worship him.

But the Israelites, obeying the laws of Moses, will not kneel down to the idol, and consequently a ruthless slaughter will follow—the greatest persecution Israel has ever undergone. During that period the Israelites who are not elected will die. But God will prepare a hiding place for the chosen Israelites, and they will remain safe for a time.

During the last three-and-a-half-year period there will be wars and rumors of wars in the world. As the oppression of the antichrist becomes unbearable, communist China will rebel against his rule. The United States will have formed a friendly relationship with China, helping her modernize her army. This army will rise in the East, pass over the Euphrates River and invade Europe. China, which has a 200-million-troop reserve army, will fight with the antichrist, and in Armageddon, or Palestine, the greatest slaughter in human history will take place. The scale of the slaughter can be imagined by the biblical image: the blood on the battleground will rise to the height of the horses' bits.

At that time the Lord will come to earth riding on a

white horse and with the saints who have ascended into heaven. He will destroy all His enemies with the sword in His mouth and He will cast the antichrist into the lake burning with fire and brimstone. The Lord will conquer the world and then the millennial kingdom will begin.

When the antichrist makes the seven-year treaty with Israel, the church of Christ will be taken up into the air. It will be spared from the Great Tribulation. Because Jesus already suffered at the cross for the judgment of sin, the church will not undergo judgment. When the antichrist makes a treaty with Israel, the news will spread throughout the world, and as the mass media spreads this news, the children of God will suddenly be taken up into heaven. While two are working in the field, one will be taken and the other left behind; two will be grinding at a mill, and one will be taken while the other is left behind.

The time will surely come when "the Lord himself shall descend from heaven with a shout, with the voice of the archangel, and with the trump of God: and the dead in Christ shall rise first" and "we which are alive and remain shall be caught up together with them in the clouds, to meet the Lord in the air: and so shall we ever be with the Lord" (1 Thess. 4:16-17). Believing that the day draws near, we should be like the wise virgins who watched and prayed as they waited for the coming of their bridegroom.

The Church at the End of the World

What will be the state of the church at the end of the world? As the end draws near, many will abandon their faith and go out to the world. "Now the Spirit speaks expressly, that in the latter times some shall depart from the faith, giving heed to seducing spirits, and doctrines

126

of devils'' (1 Tim. 4:1).

Today, many people give heed to seducing spirits and
doctrines of devils; they deny the virgin birth of Jesus,
the reality of heaven and hell; they assert that the best
way to practice true Christianity is to create a well-fed
and a well-clothed society. There are others who call
themselves Messiah, heeding the voice of devils and
possessed by deceiving spirits.

Even in such a confusion, the church, the body of
Christ, should be filled with the Holy Spirit, holding
firmly to its faith in Jesus Christ—the way, the truth and
the life. The Bible foretells that God will start the Holy
Spirit movement to adorn His bride at the end of the
world.

James says, ''Be patient, therefore, brethren, unto the
coming of the Lord. Behold, the husbandman waiteth for
the precious fruit of the earth, and hath long patience
for it, until he receive the early and latter rain. Be ye also
patient; stablish your hearts: for the coming of the Lord
draweth nigh'' (James 5:7-8).

The Holy Spirit, the early rain, was poured down in
the Upper Room on Pentecost. The latter rain, or the
fullness of the Holy Spirit, is given to us today. This latter rain began to be poured down in the early 1900s and
now, after eighty years, the work of the Holy Spirit is
carried out briskly—not only in denominations that
welcome Him openly but also in denominations that
were cold to Him. With this outpouring of the Holy
Spirit, our Lord is to adorn and take His beloved into
heaven.

And that, knowing the time, that now it is high time
to awake out of sleep: for now is our salvation nearer
than when we believed. The night is far spent, the
day is at hand: let us therefore cast off the works

127

of darkness, and let us put on the armour of light. Let us walk honestly, as in the day, not in rioting and drunkenness, not in chambering and wantonness, not in strife and envying. But put ye on the Lord Jesus Christ, and make not provision for the flesh, to fulfill the lusts thereof (Rom. 13:11-14).

We live in the time when we should watch, pray and wait. We are daily drawing closer to the moment when our hearts' cry, "Thy kingdom come," will be realized.

When you pray, "For thine is the kingdom, and the power, and the glory, for ever," envision the coming of Jesus who even now is at the door. Think about the grace of the Holy Spirit and the throne of judgment. Be grateful for the grace of God which has brought you to the last days of history. Ask what God wants you to do in this age. Think of the new heaven and the new earth along with the golden splendor of the new Jerusalem. Take thought of those brothers, relatives and neighbors who might be tormented in the Great Tribulation and cast down into the eternal hellfire because of their unbelief. Why? Because these are the thoughts of God.

Amen

In these pages we have scrutinized the deep meaning of the prayer our Lord taught us—the best and briefest prayer we can offer to God. When we accept the will and the thoughts of God contained in every phrase, when we answer them with amen, the blessing Jesus promised in the prayer will come upon us. One last time, let's review the major points of the Lord's prayer. As you do so, stop and accept each with a hearty amen.

"Our Father which art in heaven, Hallowed be thy name": God, You are among us and You have become our Father by the blood of Jesus Christ; we enjoy freedom and victory when we call You "our Father." Therefore, O Lord God, may Your name be glorified through our thinking, words and behavior. Amen—we pray that it may be done so.

"Thy kingdom come. Thy will be done in earth, as it is in heaven": We pray that Your kingdom and will may come upon our family, society and nation. Your kingdom—which Jesus brought and planted, with which Jesus filled our hearts through the Holy Spirit—is the kingdom where the sovereign power of God directs and governs our lives, making them bear fruit. In this kingdom the devils depart with a loud cry and we prosper and receive health as our souls prosper. Amen—even so, may it come true.

"Give us this day our daily bread": O God our Father, who created the material world, who sent provision to Your children in the Old Testament time, who miraculously fed Your children in the New Testament time, give us today daily bread to meet our every need. Amen—may it be done.

"And forgive us our debts, as we forgive our debtors": O God, who sent Your Son to save us from the punishment of death, we are so moved by Your great love that we forgive those who have wronged us. Forgive our sins and help us bear the cross of forgiveness with joyful hearts. Amen—may it be so done.

"Lead us not into temptation": O God our Father, help us to eat always Your Word and live in faith obeying You. Grant us Your grace that we may become faithful servants who persevere in thankfulness. Amen—help us that it may be so.

"But deliver us from evil": O God our Father, the Lucifer who was cast down into the air for rebelling and trying to usurp Your throne is incessantly trying to take us to the valley of death by sending evil spirits and demons. But because we have been able to capture the evil spirits of Satan and bind them, we are true victors. Amen—we are winners.

"Thine is the kingdom, and the power, and the glory for ever": May the new heaven and new earth, to which Jesus will lead us when He returns and breaks the force of Satan with the rod of iron, come quickly, Father.

Amen and amen.

APPENDIX

A Prayer That Is Answered

A prayer should always be answered, but if we neither expect nor receive an answer, our prayer becomes a meaningless monologue that disappears into the air. Let's analyze the kind of prayer that receives an answer. How does it work?

What Is Prayer?

Prayer is a daily dialogue between God the Father and His children. In human relationships dialogue is like respiration—when it stops, something dies. Likewise, when the dialogue of prayer is cut off between God and us, our relationship dies. Prayer is vital to our very life.

God wants to have dialogue with us. Although He

knows what we need even before we ask, He wants to listen to our need—also to our thanks and praise. David went as far as to say that God dwells in the praises of His people. I can't begin to describe the joy of such a relationship with God, of speaking to Him and then receiving an answer—whether it be tangible or in the spiritual realm.

In 1 Thessalonians 5:17, the apostle Paul said, "Pray without ceasing." Although respiration is unconscious and constant, unceasing prayer takes effort. Just how can we keep up our spiritual respiration around the clock?

To pray, we do not have to move our lips. Our thinking is prayer. If we have right thinking before God, that thinking becomes "a sweet savour" offered to the Lord. So God reads our thinking and answers it. God searches our hearts, and "he that searcheth the hearts knoweth what is the mind of the Spirit, because he maketh intercession for the saints according to the will of God" (Rom. 8:27).

If we repeat words of prayer habitually without our hearts being in it, God does not answer. When the aroma of our right thinking ascends up before God around the clock, that right thinking becomes a prayer made incessantly unto the Lord.

What is right thinking? First, let me say what it is not. It isn't a moral and ethical thinking or freedom from all worldly thought. Nor is it a stable condition of our hearts in which our thinking is kept clear like a mirror. Rather it is conditioning our thoughts to divine thoughts, as found in the Scriptures.

The Types of Prayer

When our thinking ascends before God it can take one of several forms.

132

Meditative prayer is offered through our thoughts—with our eyes open or closed, as we sit or stand, as we work or relax. But more often than not, meditative prayer is hard to offer successfully unless we are well-trained. Prayer involves concentrating our thoughts on God, and without training our thoughts are easily distracted.

Voiced prayer, in which the thoughts of our hearts are spoken aloud, has several benefits. As we speak and hear our own voice our concentration is centered and distracting thoughts are minimized. If our faith is still weak and not well-trained, it is best to verbalize our prayers, as then our prayers can reach the throne of heaven and prompt God's answer.

Our voiced prayers of praise can be sung to melodious tunes. When we praise God with an earnest and sincere heart, that praise turns into prayer. When we are not confident that we know how to pray, we can *sing praises* of thanksgiving which God honors. When Paul and Silas sang praises in the dungeon, they miraculously were delivered by the God who responded to their prayers. They'd been severely beaten and locked in jail for their testimony, yet their song arose from the depth of their hearts—and it was answered.

The Holy Spirit helps us dialogue with God. But for His help, no one could pray before God. The apostle Paul says, "No man can say that Jesus is the Lord, but by the Holy Ghost" (1 Cor. 12:3). "The Spirit itself beareth witness with our spirit, that we are the children of God" (Rom. 8:16).

We cannot call God "our Father" and pray before Him until the Holy Spirit helps us. But the Holy Spirit can also take our prayer to an even higher level. When we are filled with the Holy Spirit, God's grace makes us speak in languages we didn't learn naturally; the Spirit loosens our tongue. "For he that speaketh in an unknown tongue speaketh not unto men, but unto God: for no man understandeth him: howbeit in the spirit he speaketh mysteries" (1 Cor. 14:2).

As we pray not only with our learned human language but in a prayer language as the Holy Spirit leads us, He helps us overcome restrictions placed upon us by time and space. He takes us into a deeper grace of God. One of my close friends, Rev. Bailus, told me his own story which shows the power of prayer when the Spirit joins with our spirit and brings before God situations of which we're not even aware.

One Sunday Rev. Bailus was eating lunch with his family when the Holy Spirit commanded him to pray. The urge was so strong that he left the table and went to his prayer room where he prayed in tongues with such fervency that he sweat all over. He didn't know what he was burdened about but after praying about half an hour, his peace returned. He felt free to finish his lunch and then he followed his Sunday afternoon routine: He went to a cookie shop at the nearby streetcar terminal.

The shopkeeper seemed surprised to see him and reported that Rev. Bailus's parents had been involved in a traffic accident—at the very hour when he'd felt compelled to pray in tongues. When Rev. Bailus reached the scene of the accident, he found their Volkswagen crushed flat against a truck loaded with building materials. He was sure his parents could not have survived. And then a police officer standing beside the crushed car commented, "I haven't seen such a miracle in my twenty years on the police force. In this kind of accident, everyone is always crushed to death under the truck, but these two elderly people were pushed out—as if somebody had held them in his arms."

Rev. Bailus rushed to the hospital, where he found his

parents lying on beds, safe except for a few scratches.

As my friend learned, the Holy Spirit can lead us to pray about problems we can't even identify—until we see the results of our heart's intercession in the Spirit.

The Purpose of Prayer

Through prayer, *we can graft the divine mind to our minds.*

Jesus said, "Repent," and the original word means, "Change your thought and emotion!" We must change our negative thoughts and receive the richness, forgiveness, love and mercy that are in God. The Bible says, "Let this mind be in you, which was also in Christ Jesus" (Phil. 2:5). When we accept divine thoughts in our minds through the Scriptures and offer these thoughts back to God, the mind of God is miraculously grafted in our minds. When this happens we are able to possess divine power. God is able to do what is humanly impossible. God is love and we are beneficiaries of that love. God gives grace and we receive it. God is health and we live in it. God is wealth and we enjoy it.

Through prayer we can also *be assured of the remission of our sins.* We should pray as Jonah did—that our sins may be forgiven. When Jonah fled to Tarshish against God's divine commandment and encountered the judgment of God, he repented thoroughly before the Lord. "And thou heardest my voice. For thou hadst cast me into the deep, in the midst of the seas; and the floods compassed me about: all thy billows and thy waves passed over me. Then I said, I am cast out of thy sight; yet I will look again toward thy holy temple" (Jon. 2:2-4).

To the people of Israel, turning one's face toward the temple symbolized repentance. Our sins are forgiven when we confess them and repent before God, whose very nature is love and forgiveness. "Come now, and let us reason together, saith the Lord: though your sins be as scarlet, they shall be as white as snow; though they be red like crimson, they shall be as wool" (Is. 1:18).

Through prayer we can also be assured that God has forgiven our original sin and presumptuous sins with the blood of Jesus Christ. The devil always whispers the lie that we Christians are still in sin, that we must surely pay the price of sin. But God never remembers the sin He once forgave. God recognized us as people who have never committed a sin against Him. We are justified by faith. This is true. So why are we still haunted by our guilty conscience? Because we don't pray with thanksgiving and accept the forgiveness of God and the power of the blood of Jesus. Prayer assures us that we are forgiven of our sins; it provides us with new energy to live boldly as a righteous person.

Prayer also opens our eyes to eternal life. Our Lord is "the Lord the maker thereof, the Lord that formed it, to establish it" (Jer. 33:2). God sent His Son, Jesus Christ, to this world so that whoever believes in Him shall not perish, but have eternal life (John 3:16). That eternal life does not merely mean that we will live forever. Even those who go to hell for their sin of unbelief and for living in sin will live endlessly—in torment.

The eternal life we inherit is the life of our heavenly Father. It is the blessed life we enjoy even now, in this world. When we graft our minds into God's mind and offer prayer to glorify Him, the overflowing peace and joy in our hearts open our eyes to eternal things. This peace and joy are proof that the Spirit of God is within us.

What else does prayer do? *It lightens the burdens of life.*

Nobody lives in this world without being laden with burdens, though each person's weight differs from another's. But Jesus said, "Come unto me, all ye that labor and are heavy laden, and I will give you rest" (Matt. 11:28). How can we come to Jesus? Through prayer. When we lay down our burdens before Jesus, the Holy Spirit, who is sent by Jesus, will solve them.

Through prayer, our diseases are also healed. Disease exists because of our direct or indirect sins. If we believe in Jesus as our Savior, however, we should be set free from sickness—as well as forgiven of our sins. It is His divine will that we live in health till we are called to heaven. Jesus spent most of His public ministry healing the sick. The Bible reads, "With His stripes we are healed" (Is. 53:5). When we thus come to God, praying with unswerving faith, like the New Testament Syrophenician woman or the Roman centurion, we can be delivered from the grip of sickness.

The way to *resist the devil and put him to flight* is through our prayer. Satan was already defeated on the cross. His defeat will be completed at the end of the Great Tribulation when he is bound. Accordingly, we must take the devil captive by the power and merit of the blood of Jesus; as we fast and pray we are able to resist the devil.

Through prayer we can overcome trials.

Our prayer is essential if we are not to fall into temptation; it is indispensable if we are to be delivered from the midst of temptation. The night Jesus was betrayed, He said to His disciples in the Garden of Gethsemane, "Why sleep ye? Rise and pray, lest ye enter into temptation" (Luke 22:46). If those disciples had prayed at that time instead of falling asleep, what would have happened? Peter might not have denied Jesus. The best way to get out of temptation is not to make excuses or to avenge ourselves, but to fall down before the Lord, humble ourselves and pray.

Approaching God

General prayer gives glory to God, gives Him thanks, confesses daily sins, reports to Him what has happened in our daily lives and asks Him for our daily needs. General prayer concerns the day-in and day-out routines of life. In a general fashion, we should praise God for His grace and redemption. We should pray constantly for the help of God in everything that touches our everyday lives, especially for the well-being of our spiritual lives, our health and our business lives.

But special prayer is offered when we are faced with an urgent problem or decision. If we want to find the will of God or have an answer to a problem, such as sickness or material need, we must pray to God with a special resolution and attitude. How do we do that?

First, we must clarify the object—in detail. If we don't have a definite need for which we are praying, we cannot know if God has answered our prayer. In addition, the prayer that is not specific is not usually accompanied by a burning desire that makes us persistent.

When the disciples of Jesus asked Him, "Lord, teach us to pray, as John also taught his disciples" (Luke 11:1), Jesus told them this parable:

> Which of you shall have a friend, and shall go unto him at midnight, and say unto him, Friend, lend me three loaves: for a friend of mine in his journey is come to me, and I have nothing to set before him? And he from within shall answer and say, Trouble me not: the door is shut, and my children are with me in bed; I cannot rise and give thee (Luke 11:5-7).

When the man in this story came to his friend, he did not say, "Lend me bread," or "Lend me a few loaves."

He explained the situation concretely in which he needed the bread and said, "Lend me three loaves." Our prayers also should have such definite details.

All the prayers mentioned in the Bible have explicit and definite objectives. Genesis 24 recounts Abraham's prayer offered when he sent his servant to find a wife for Isaac. Its contents are quite concrete, as is the prayer of Gideon recorded in the sixth chapter of Judges. When we plan our prayer requests it is good to ask ourselves a threefold question: "What is our request?" "How much is our request?" and "When do we want our request to be answered?"

Second, our prayers must be based on the Word of God. However specific our requests, if they are against the will of God, they cannot be answered. So when we pray to God, we must approach Him with His Word. Is our request contrary to the will of God? The apostle Paul says, "And be not conformed to this world: but be ye transformed by the renewing of your mind, that ye may prove what is that good, and acceptable, and perfect, will of God" (Rom. 12:2).

The Word of God shows us what is "that good, and acceptable, and perfect, will of God." It is His divine will that we become healthy, that we prosper, that we be set free from a guilty conscience.

Third, we must offer the prayer of repentance and forgiveness. If I harbor iniquity in my heart, God neither hears nor answers my prayer (Ps. 66:18). Sin always becomes a wall between God and us. It obstructs our prayer from coming up before God; it blocks God's answer from coming down to us.

Jesus said that we should first forgive the sins and trespasses of our neighbors, "For if ye forgive men their trespasses, your heavenly Father will also forgive you" (Matt. 6:14-15).

Therefore I say unto you, What things soever ye desire, when ye pray, believe that ye receive them, and ye shall have them. And when ye stand praying, forgive, if ye have ought against any: that your Father also which is in heaven may forgive you your trespasses (Mark 11:24-25).

Fourth, we should have the faith of God. When Jesus' disciples were astonished to see a withered fig tree which He had cursed, Jesus said to them:

Have faith in God. For verily I say unto you, That whosoever shall say unto this mountain, Be thou removed, and be thou cast into the sea; and shall not doubt in his heart, but shall believe that those things which he saith shall come to pass; he shall have whatsoever he saith (Mark 11:23).

In the original Greek, the expression "Have faith in God" is really "Have the faith of God," which is differentiated from the general faith or natural belief we have. The faith of God is shed in our hearts by the Holy Spirit when we read the Word. Once this faith enters our hearts, we can firmly believe even what is not possible in the light of reason. What causes this faith in our hearts is just *rhema*, "because greater is he that is in you, than he that is in the world" (1 John 4:4). When we receive the faith of God by His Word and by the help of the Holy Spirit, a miracle takes place. Satan, who has the power of the air, departs from us when God's Word dwells within us, and Satan's grip over our environment is loosened.

Fifth, we must ask for the help of the Holy Spirit who is at our side to help us. He knows our need and He knows our desire. He also knows God's will and the answer God has prepared for us.

> For what man knoweth the things of a man, save the
> spirit of man which is in him? Even so the things of
> God knoweth no man, but the Spirit of God. Now
> we have received, not the spirit of the world, but
> the spirit which is of God; that we might know the
> things that are freely given to us of God (1 Cor.
> 2:11-12).

When we depend upon the Spirit of God we can move
swiftly like a bird that rides upon wind toward the place
where the answer of God awaits us.

Sixth, we should pray with a burning desire. He who
doesn't pray with a burning desire cannot receive
anything. Jesus told us a parable of a poor widow and
a heartless judge to teach that we should pray resolutely
and not faint. The earnest attitude of the Syrophenician
woman is the very attitude of prayer that we should learn
(Matt. 15:21-28).

How long should we pray with a burning heart? We
should pray until we are assured of the answer, until we
have peace and joy. If we arise saying, "Lord, I believe,"
without the assurance that our prayer has been answered,
our prayer is one-sided; God is not bound. When the
answer is on the way, the Holy Spirit comes to us with
a peaceful assurance. "Be careful for nothing; but in every
thing by prayer and supplication with thanksgiving let
your requests be made known unto God. And the peace
of God, which passeth all understanding, shall keep your
hearts and minds through Christ Jesus" (Phil. 4:6-7).

Seventh, once we have the assurance in our hearts, we
should cease praying for the request and start offering
prayers of thanksgiving, confessing with our mouths and
saying with faith, "Health shall come to me." "Material

wealth shall come to me." "My children shall obey me."

Whatever we ask, we should confess the assurance that the Spirit gives us and boldly command the answer to take place. This great declaration causes a creative work to happen in our surroundings.